Jim Eiting's
WINE TIMES

11 - 4 - 17

all the best,

Jim

Jim Eiting's
WINE TIMES

Food, Fun, Friends, and Family

James A. Eiting

ORANGE *frazer* PRESS
Wilmington, Ohio

Published for the author by:
Orange Frazer Press
P.O. Box 214
Wilmington, OH 45177
Telephone: 937.382.3196 for price and shipping information.
Website: www.orangefrazer.com

Book and cover design: Alyson Rua and Orange Frazer Press

Library of Congress Control Number: 2016963306

First Printing

The cover art was painted by Charice Morel, a dear friend and
neighbor, who is a very successful artist. Our Santa Barbara proper-
ties actually touch, but only slightly.

Their wonderful home is the location of the tiny Compañeros
Winery of which her husband, retired radiologist, Art Morel, is one-
third owner. The winery is at the lower portion of their 100-year-old
carriage house, with Charice and her studio being on the first level.

The watch is to remind us that time is a most precious commod-
ity and also to signify that wine stored in a bottle is not wasted. It is
a gift to you to make good wine even better.

The candle signifies illumination. Hopefully you will gain much
knowledge as you peruse the book.

Acknowledgments

I have been helped by so many wonderful people and experiences. It is futile to try to name them all!

Nevertheless, I must mention Todd Dammeyer, Mike and Carol Williams of the Winery at Versailles, the members of Vino Versailles (our wine group), Art and Charice Morel, and Antonio Gardella. They have all added a lot of perspective to the wine section.

Important, too, is my wife Esther who patiently worked with me as we added recipes that stand out in our mind as being worthy of mention.

Thanks to the people who took the time to read my manuscript. They are: Todd Dammeyer, Mike and Telisa Deligatta, Mike Williams, Antonio Gardella, Art Morel, Jim Raterman, Dave Newton, Chris Chirgwin, John Klamar, Bob Chelle, Michelle Rasch, and Ernie Ettorre.

They were all asked to read my *opus* and I really appreciated their input. Each was chosen for a different reason and that makes their contribution that much more important. Lucky, I am!

I have learned much from the following people: Lettie Teague of the *Wall Street Journal*, James Laube, Matt Kremer, James Molesworth, Dr. Vinifera (Vinny), and from *Wine Spectator* magazine (one of my favorites). A special thanks to the people at Orange Frazer. They are bright, easy to work with, very helpful, and creative.

Contents

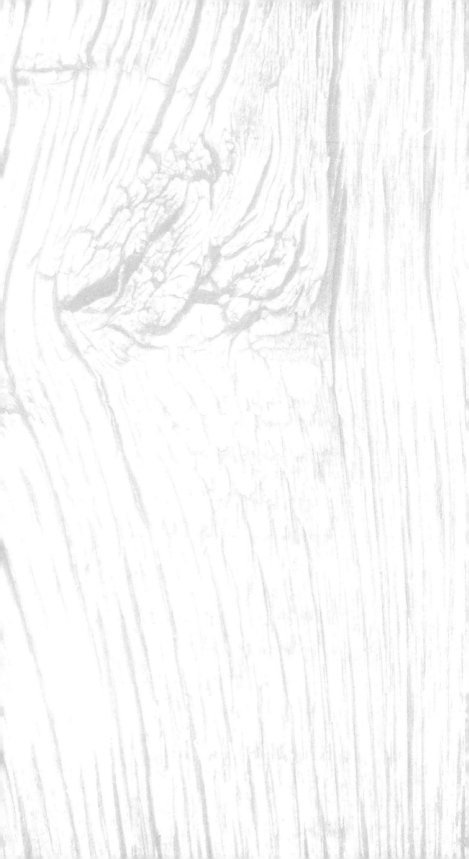

☙ FOREWORD

Mention the word wine to people and you will probably get many different responses. From thoughts of cheap liquor to lavish Roman dinners, wine and its enjoyment have been with us for thousands of years.

Unfortunately, there are few who have the opportunity to wander a the vineyard. So we learn as we go. For sure, author Jim Eiting has boldly entered the vineyard. He has developed a great knowledge about and an appreciation for wines. We are fortunate that he shares this with those who wish to learn.

Many of us have witnessed the common journey of a nascent wine explorer. It might begin by purchasing modestly priced wines to more expensive wines to subscribing to *Wine Spectator* to attending formal classes and, perhaps the crescendo, to building and painstakingly stocking your own wine cellar for the enjoyment of family and friends.

Jim Eiting has a deliberate sense of style. Whether it is clothing, travel, or a glass of a rare Cabernet, he delights in examining things, separating into parts, testing and then developing explanations of how something works. Sometimes things don't work well and other times, there is complete harmony. So it is with wine.

How it works is important to Jim. He says that the same bottle of wine could taste differently under different conditions: food, temperature, time of day, mood, and venue all play important parts in the ritual of drinking wine. Whether it be simply 'throwing it back' or decanting to perfection then combining with great attention to food pairing, the challenges of drinking wine are many.

If you are just putting your toe into the vast ocean of the wine world, or if you are an expert who has become one by reading and drinking and reading more and drinking more, this book has something for everyone. Once again, thank you Jim Eiting.

Your friend and fellow wine aficionado,
Bob Chelle

❧ PREFACE

This is not a wine book, but a book about wine, its enjoyment, and easy gourmet recipes. I believe a person only needs a few wine varietals to feel happy with life. We do not have the time today to devote to a lot of reading. The internet changed our reading habits. Thus, it has been my goal to share my knowledge with you in an abridged format. Besides, people want to enjoy wine, not to be an encyclopedia about it.

An oenophile (wine pro) can be both intimidating and boring. Most people simply want to enjoy wine, and can do quite well with a limited amount of knowledge.

This book is biased as, after thirty years of enjoying wine, I have distilled my favorites down to very few varietals. Rest assured, it has been very enjoyable educating myself. California cabernets do get center stage, as I feel they have earned it! But, then so has Bordeaux worldwide, for an eternity.

I do not claim originality. My writing is the result of reading and absorbing twenty-five books about wine, reading hundreds of wine articles, and attending as many wine classes as I could. Add to that, great input from a few knowledgeable friends and our wine club, Vino Versailles, named after the Versailles, Ohio, community in which we domicile. In addition, we have learned much on our international travels.

We have lived in small towns our entire lives but have traveled widely. We and our children enjoy our dogs, modest homes, small cars, and no swimming pools. But we all enjoy our wine cellars and wine friends.

Esther and I were very fortunate to discover Santa Barbara, California, twenty-five years ago and enjoy the climate of good wine and friends there. Writing this book has been a natural progression of our quarter century there. In addition, my brother Jack, and his wife Marie, live in Oregon where they grow Pinot Noir and Pinot Gris and they have been very kind in sharing cases of it with us. Are we lucky, or what?

Wine Times was written not for coin, but to summarize our experiences and learning, and to share our deep love for the grape and the enjoyment it brings to mankind.

Friend and city college teacher Antonio Gardella says it perfectly: "Wine is magic. Wherever you find fine wine, you find fine art and great people!"

Me with my siblings in Colorado.

❧ OUR INTRODUCTION TO WINE

We got to Santa Barbara, California, about thirty years ago where we bought a second home. As CEO of Midmark Corporation, I belonged to an organization called Young Presidents (an organization for people who were presidents before they were forty years old). We belonged to a chapter in the Midwest. You must leave Young Presidents when you turn fifty. Then, there is a following group called World Presidents, which is a great worldwide fraternity and the members help each other through idea exchange. It has been extremely helpful to Esther and me.

After getting settled in Santa Barbara, we met a couple, Ed and Eve Savage, who are dear friends to this day. He informed me that they were setting up a World Presidents chapter in Santa Barbara and asked if I would be interested in joining. We said yes, as we knew no one in Santa Barbara.

We went to our first event which was held outside at a palatial home. I went up to the bar (which was in a tent) and ordered a beer, which was what I drank at the time, and was told they had none. Esther was a scotch drinker so I ordered one for her and again was told they had none. So at that moment we became wine drinkers and have been so ever since, with no regrets! California is wine country. Believe me!

Jim Eiting's
WINE TIMES

1

Wine, a Synopsis

Bacchus, Roman god of wine.

🍷 HISTORY OF WINE

The bible supports the thesis that the original site of wine-making is the general area of the Caucasus which is the area between the Black Sea and the Caspian Sea. This puts it in the countries of Georgia, Azerbaijan, etc. However, the original dating of the first recorded wine-making is Egypt in 5400 B.C. The oldest bottle of wine was opened in London in 1961. It was 421 years old and a German white, surprisingly good when opened, but quickly turned to vinegar once hit by the air. America's first winery was founded in 1773.

CREATION OF WINE

All wines start as grape juice, hopefully from good grapes. In the process, sugar is directly converted to ethyl alcohol. Yeast is a major ingredient. Thus, the vintner will determine what kind of wine is to be made and also the amount of sugar (brix) they will want at harvest. Bear in mind that grapes have the highest sugar content of all fruit, even substantially higher than sugar cane or beets, at the time of harvest. Important, too, is the pH, which represents the amount of acidity and alkalinity. This will determine the longevity of red wine.

The juices of both red and white wine are colorless. The difference is in the skins. Thus, fermenting the juice and the skins together is what creates a red wine.

The vintner must also determine whether to ferment in stainless steel or oak barrels. Sometimes bagged oak chips may be used to give it an oaky flavor. Oak barrels impart a distinctive flavor and usually not used for white wine except for Chardonnay. Most other whites use stainless steel tanks only.

The stainless tanks are glycol jacketed for temperature control. This allows for better quality control and improved economics as well.

The vintner monitors the fermentation carefully and samples it daily. They are striving for balance between tannins, acidity, sugar, and alcohol. Most wines are allowed to ferment until all the sugar is converted to alcohol.

Some wines are filtered to remove impurities, but when you do, you begin to lose texture. Also, the more you work a wine with things like filtration, additives, etc., it begins to lose its originality. Less is better always.

As consumers, do not be concerned about sulfites as they do occur naturally in all wines and other foods. They are actually inorganic salts produced as a bi-product of the fermentation process.

The amount of desired color in reds is determined by the amount of time the skins are in the fermenting wine. Might I add that darker red wines seem to have more body but that is a personal observation.

🐚 WINE KNOWLEDGE

Let me start by mentioning that I have not researched other schools, but the University of California at Davis has a specific viticulture and oenology program which has been referred to as the Harvard of Wine Making. Quite renowned and yet tiny, they graduate approximately 100 people per year.

Wine making is truly an art form for good wines and the makers have to have a very sensitive palate. They almost have to be born into the industry. Blending requires a great deal of experience to get the combination just right.

University of California at Davis is very helpful and a truly good classroom education, but they also insist that the students have hands-on experience from planting through the autumn harvest crush. In spite of the above, one can become a class wine-maker without a formal education. Today, that has become very rare due to the technology acceleration, as in other fields as well.

A midwest farmer is much the same. Although they can succeed without a formal degree, education is vital today with the increase in new information and techniques. This said, being born into it is a precious experience second to none.

🍇 AGING

Yes, the great Bordeaux's of France do attain some of their greatness by aging. But today, with improved education and technology, personal cellars are less for aging and more for storage, convenience, and conversation. And, looking at the entire world, less than one percent of all wines are designed to age.

Like people, wine starts by being young and energetic. At some point, they mature and remain that way for years. But eventually, like people, time catches up to them and they become old and frail. Where is that point?

Today, most stored wines do not improve greatly, so do not overdo the storage thing. And never forget, there are no guarantees in life, so open it now and enjoy it with certainty. I feel the same, uncategorically, about possessions and children. Give now so your children can enjoy the gift and you can enjoy the thrill of giving.

I do not recommend long aging. Some aging may be good, but too much can actually cause decline in wine flavors as reds go from purple to brick color. Never forget that once the fruit leaves the vines, their flavors begin their decline, thus when to open a wine gets rather dicey.

My personal rules for aging are as follows:

Keep bottles away from vibration or movement. From Antonio Gardella, "Think of wine as a baby. It can't stand shaking and moving. It is hard on it."

Store it in a dark, cool place away from any sunlight or anything that would cause temperature spikes.

Fifty-five degrees is ideal but a constant sixty-five degrees is adequate. Seventy degrees is just too warm and too cold inhibits the softening of the tannins which you want to fall into the background. Ideal humidity is thirty percent.

Keep bottles on their sides or upside down to keep corks moist and to prevent oxidation.

Finally, my personal ten-year rule: Do not keep anything beyond ten years unless it is a very expensive Bordeaux or from a special event. Wine is like a river. It moves constantly and is never the same as it passes by you. Six years is ideal.

This has nothing to do with aging, but I have found white wines that are opened can last a very long time if refrigerated. Reds however, can hold twenty-four hours if opened and kept refrigerated. If left opened and unrefrigerated, they will taste like they have been filtered through coffee grounds.

In spite of all the above, and poetically, "old violins make the sweetest music."

OUR WINE CELLARS

Let me preface this section by stating that I have read and re-read that the following are ideal temperatures for serving different wines:

Champagne	50 degrees
Whites and Rosés	55 degrees
Dessert Wines	60 degrees
Reds	65 degrees

That being said, when we built our home in Ohio, Esther wanted rain water for doing her clothes washing. In building the home, we thought it would look best with a shake shingle roof and it did. Well, when the basement was poured with concrete, it included a 15' x 40' cistern. It slowly filled with rain water and to our chagrin, the roof water picked up a dye from the shake shingles, making the water a light brown,

Our wine cellar in Versailles, Ohio.

unsuitable for washing. So, we drained the cistern and put in a water softener, which worked well.

In the ensuing years, I fell in love with wine and one evening, lying in bed, I thought, what an ideal wine cellar! So, we cut a hole in the basement wall, added a door, put in a concave false brick ceiling and laid a real brick floor. We added period light fixtures, a tapestry, shelves, and a wine

table made from a wine barrel. It has worked superbly, and we have fun not only storing our wines in it, but also inviting couples down to sit around the wine barrel table and open a wine for the evening.

Our next cellar was in Santa Barbara, California, where we have a home built into a hillside that overlooks the ocean. The garage is built beneath the home and has a small cellar inside of it. Again, we lucked out, and built a wine cabinet into the cellar there. It held its temperature at a perfect sixty-five degrees and has worked so well.

Then, twelve years ago, we purchased a home on the Catawba Peninsula at Lake Erie. It was built over a crawl space and had a trap door in the pantry that you could access it from, with a four-step ladder permanently in place. So, we put some shelves down there, and I put down large carpet strips where you could crawl into the shelf area, which again, provided a perfect sixty-five degrees.

So there you are, three wonderful wine areas with a perfect temperature, no light, and no vibration.

Our wine cellar in Santa Barbara, California.

ALCOHOL PERCENTAGES

I am of the school that thinks that alcohol percentages do not necessarily make a wine better. Wine is all about relaxation, fellowship, and conversation, and not getting overly imbibed.

Alcohol does deliver flavor, somewhat like the fat in marbleized beef, and alcohol percentages are averaging up, but there is a limit which I feel we have reached. Many sommeliers do not like to get over fourteen percent and I understand why. You want a balanced wine. Fortunately, the percentages seem to have peaked and are going down.

In the wine process, as grapes ripen, they accumulate sugar, which in the fermentation process, is converted to alcohol. And that sugar comes from *hang time* or late sunny harvests. But higher alcohol content does create a bigger flavor and tends to win more wine contests.

The *legs* or *church windows* on the inside of your glass are actually the alcohol content and are fun to see.

In my experience, the cutoff point is thirteen-and-a-half percent but I am very comfortable at twelve-and-a-half percent as well. In fact, I can actually feel the difference between twelve and fourteen percent when sharing a bottle of wine. With the lower percentages I am always happier as you stay much more in control of your conversation and driving.

Yet, when having a very small glass of port after a meal, I am comfortable as well. As I know that twenty percent is a given with port and therefore, sip very slowly and enjoy every drop.

And this final note, hangovers (spent too much time in the vineyard) do not necessarily come from the sugar or alcohol percentage, but dehydration. Always pair wine with water in equal percentages.

🐾 OAK TREES

The oak used in the best barrels can come from certain French oak trees that impart a vanilla flavor that are used only three times for the best newly fermented wines. But subsequent to that, the barrels can then be used as a neutral storage for other wines, for up to twenty-five years. The oak used in these barrels is dried for two years before using it for new barrels. That is to leach out the saps and tars.

🐾 CORKS

The most popular of all corks come from the bark of the cork oak tree. They grow in the poor rocky soil of southern Portugal and Spain. The material that comes from the bark has the ability to mold itself to the sometimes imperfect diameter of the bottle neck, thus getting a good seal. Historically, the longest corks were used for the best wines.

The negative of natural cork is that they can split or crumble after ten years or so, or even leak. Personally, like the wine itself, I feel the combination of the two are reliable for about ten years. Also, there is a wine term called corked that is the musty smell. This is noticed upon opening a bottle. It actually reminds you of the odor of wet cardboard. Although not harmful, it does take away from the nose of the wine.

As you may have noticed, artificial corks made from recycled plastic are definitely on the rise and rightly so, as they do not deteriorate and you do not even have to lay the bottle down to keep the cork moist.

Twist offs are definitely on the rise, but people seem to feel that they relate to plonk wines. Personally, I feel there is a certain romance in pulling the cork and hearing the familiar pop upon the opening of the wine. It is almost ceremonial.

&. DECANTING

Let me start by saying that you always stand a bottle up for twenty-four hours before opening it. That is to let the sediment go to the bottom of the bottle.

Decanting is all about breathing and wine cannot breathe in its own bottle. Breathing is all about exposure to oxygen, and that, too, is why you swirl the wine in its glass. In addition to giving it more nose, it exposes it to more oxygen. This will help in softening the tannins and acid and actually improve the flavor. Three hours in a wide-mouthed container can do wonders. Never forget wine is a living thing. Oxygen is the saving key. Wine needs oxygen to grow, oxygen to ferment, and oxygen to age. Oxygen is life itself. Like a river, wine is a constantly moving thing.

🍷 FLAVOR

Bear in mind that everyone's taste and smell receptors are different. No two are the same.

The most important component of wine is the quality of the grapes. Without that, nothing else matters. In growing, they pick up their surroundings—the soil, sun, slope, etc. The resulting wine should have a sense of place and offer a passionate, singular vision, not its component parts. For example, oak, vanilla, alcohol, etc.

The grape begins its decline once it leaves the vine. It is important to move them quickly! The flavor of the grape is right next to its skin. Overripe is much better for flavor as the grape will have less water, more color, and more tannins. Acid is important too. It gives the wine snap. Without it, the wine is flabby.

Heavily influenced by smell, one must appreciate that there are probably 1,000 components in a wine, each having its own taste, and thus a very complex fluid. Wine ends up being so many things at once. Chemistry, climate, soil, sun, farming, geography, and many others not even mentioned.

Wine is an art and not a science. The winemakers' task is flavor-balance. Major flavor drivers such as sweetness, acidity, oak, etc. must be so well integrated that they are almost imperceptible. You want your acid, fruit, and tannins to blend.

The psychology of wine is also so complex. It also has to do with that particular row of grapes, storage, and also the mood of the person opening the bottle. If you do have a special bottle, make sure the time is right for you as you do not know when it is the perfect time for that bottle.

If you have a restaurant house wine some night and you really enjoy the people you are with, the table cloths are right, wonderful smells coming from the kitchen and the food is delicious and you ask the wine label and order a case, don't be surprised if you are disappointed upon opening the case because the gestalt of wine is very psychological.

Remember, a great painting might look different to you today than it did ten years ago. Did the painting change or did you? Wine does change color but so does your taste, mood, and circumstances. A great flavor can be gone in six months. So live in the moment. A great wine gives you not only flavor, but emotion, too.

🍷 TASTING THE WINE

Let me begin by stating that everyone's taste and smell receptors are different. No two are alike.

People perceive four basic tastes: sweet, sour, bitter, and salt. It is important to know that our tastes are driven seventy percent by smell, which is why it is crucial to take a big whiff of the wine from a wide-mouth wine glass before you even taste it. Our sense of smell is able to discern over 1,000 different odors. Therefore, if at a serious wine tasting, never wear perfume or aftershave lotion. They will tip over the whole program, not only for the wearer but also the people around them.

To add to that, when you are at an event and cheese is served with pepper on it as an appetizer, it will tip over your taste buds and prevent you from having a good accurate taste of the wine. To bring that home, each evening, I have a small glass of port with stilton cheese. The salt flavor in some stiltons will overpower the taste of the port. In my situation, salt is the flavor I taste first, always.

THE SIX S's ARE IMPORTANT

1 **See**—Look at the color. Is it intense or flabby? Dull or bright? Allow a long-aged red to have a brick color. That is very natural.

2 **Swirl**—Swirl your glass and look like a pro. That is another reason to have a large glass. The wine on the sides of the glass will release more of the smell.

3 **Sniff**—Do you smell an intense flavor? Or is it a "nonevent" instead?

4 **Sip**—Take a small sip and swish it around in your mouth so all of your taste buds feel it. Hold it in your mouth for a few seconds so you can feel the texture and balance. Remember, you drink beer, but you sip wine.

5 **Swallow**—Does it truly have a pleasing taste? The finish of a wine is what you taste in the next ninety seconds. This is the moment of truth to test all the adjectives you read on the label.

6 **Spit**—If at a wine tasting, there should always be a spit bucket to do this and not be embarrassed. It is a standard of the industry and has prevented many DUI's and embarrassing situations.

Worthy of mention here is complexity. A complex wine has many aromas and flavors. It is layered and nuanced. Nothing about it is simple or straightforward. It keeps unfolding in your glass, revealing more and more scents as you slowly sip it.

This does not mean that straightforward wines are not good. They are called fruit forward or new world wines as in the wines that are from California, Chile, and Australia. Old world wines, like France or Italy, are earth driven or subtly flavored like earth and oak. Much of that is driven by the amount of sun the grapevines receive.

As I grow older, I put more of a premium on the depth and complexity of a wine, than on the forwardness perhaps of a fruit forward

See

Swirl

Sniff

Sip

Swallow

Spit

wine. And as you too, move forward into better wine, I am sure you will agree.

Finally, wine is the world's most sensuous drink. You have to see, smell, taste, and savor.

TANNINS

If you have ever bitten into a grape seed, that bitter taste is tannin.

Tannins (polyphenols) are needed, or wines cannot age. It is only in red wines, and it comes from the skins and stems of the grapes. It is the spine of a good wine. They are needed and are a preservative. They rarely fade away completely, which is good.

They cause a sensation of astringency in the mouth (pucker). If a wine has loads of fruit and alcohol but inadequate tannins, it will lack definition. It can be high in some young wines.

Cabernet Sauvignon would have the greatest concentration of tannins, and Pinot Noir, the least. Merlot would be somewhere in between. Generally, darker colored wines will be higher in tannins.

If a wine's tannins are especially high, cellar it for a year or so. Barrel aging does reduce the tannin level the most, as a small amount of oxygen is introduced through the barrel aging process. But it can be further reduced by bottle aging. That will help develop its elegance and complexity.

HEADACHE

Headache? "Wandered too far into the vineyard?"

Wine is a wonderful and pleasurable way of bringing people together for great conversation. Here are some good pointers for you:

Inexpensive wines many times have too much sugar added to boost the amount of alcohol content. This causes pain! California does not allow sugar to be added.

A headache the next day comes from dehydration while consuming wine. Make absolutely certain that you match every sip of wine with an equal sip of water.

Drinking even a modest amount of wine without eating some food with it, is a great way to feel rotten. Cheese is a great friend of wine drinkers.

Never, ever be the first one to arrive at a party or the last one to leave. And never ever be both.

WINE GLASSES

Bear in mind that wine taste is seventy percent driven by the smell you receive from it. In fact, we have some friends who have lost their sense of smell and have never felt enjoying wine was the same. With that in mind, swirling the glass is so important and that accents the reason for the importance of the shape of the glass. Also, always hold the glass by the stem so you do not change the wine temperature.

With that in mind, think of a wine glass shape as a very large egg with the top third lopped off. Definitely a curved in glass and the thinner the glass, the better. The thinner glass just gives the wine a nicer feel.

Might I add that too many wines suffer from too small of a glass. Getting your nose into the glass is very important in picking up all the flavors.

In view of that, a glass should always be less than half full. And a bottle should yield four or five pours so it gives you some idea of what the glass size should be. Never forget, you drink beer, but you sip wine.

Have a napkin at the neck of the bottle and then turn the bottle slightly when finished pouring so the napkin catches the last drop. And never, ever, turn the bottle upside down when the bottle is empty. The bottom is where the residuals lie and you will look like an amateur if you do.

When drinking aperitifs, ports, etc. a small glass is always used since the volume is so tiny.

For sparkling wines, a flute should always be used. Like sparkling, they are to signify that it is a special event.

🎵 OPEN-THAT-BOTTLE-NIGHT

In 1999, someone got the idea to make one special wine night a year. It is always the fourth Saturday in February. It is a worldwide evening.

That is a night when you open your special bottle of wine that you have been saving. It could be from a graduation, wedding anniversary, birthday, or even a great vacation. It should be a bottle that holds a cherished memory from your lives. And if you do not have one, purchase an upscale one for that evening, something you normally would not buy for yourself.

Many people have Open-That-Bottle-Night parties or perhaps just meet some good friends at a restaurant and upon opening your bottle, share the memory of it with the people who join you.

Should you meet at a restaurant with your bottle of wine, expect to pay a corkage fee. Restaurants charge between $15 and $50 should you bring your own bottle.

NÉGOCIANTS

Estate bottled is a wonderful and beguiling term that even has some romance in it.

But, today things are much different. So many grapes are contracted for by good and bad wine labels. It simply makes a lot of sense and it even lessens the dangers of being tied down to a potential bad harvest.

An example is a class label who had contracted from a known grape source and produces a wonderful wine. But fortunately, sometimes there is an overrun and they end up with more than they need. Also, they want to keep their case count down, so that they are able to keep their price category where they want it.

This is an important comment from Mike Williams, the very successful owner of the Winery at Versailles. It is on blending:

> "When blending, one must not only keep the weakness of the wine to be blended, but the future development of that wine in mind. By trying to fill the hole in a wine with blending wines, one must consider all the factors of the blending wine…i.e. in trying to add additional color to a wine that is otherwise well-structured, you

can add too much fruit and cover subtle flavors. The key is to always add layers of flavor and add to the complexity. We've added wines to prop up an otherwise good wine by blending seemingly lower class wines that had the needed element."

Therefore, they will sell the overrun to a less classic label, priced right, who are more than pleased at the opportunity.

So how do we as consumers find these bargains? My comment here is to know a good smaller wine store and speak to the people there who are probably aware of the situations. This does not happen in supermarkets.

A good example of a class Négociants would be Cameron Hughes.

🐌 RATING

Robert Parker's book *Wine Buyer's Guide* had the greatest impact on me with this subject. I found him to be very honest and forthright in his assessment of wines. He pulled no punches and was not affected by advertising dollars that affect others. So many times, a rating is skewed by the amount an advertiser is spending which has to affect the person doing the rating.

On his 100-point scale, Parker gave everyone a score of fifty points just for showing up. Then he rated the wine and percentages on:

Color—5 points
Aroma or bouquet—15 points
Flavor and finish—20 points
Overall—10 points

This nets out to:
64–74 average
75–79 above average
80–90 very good (a great area for your great value price)
91–95 outstanding (superior character and style)
96–100 exemplary (a classic wine)

Finally, this from Robert Parker's great book when he described the 1982 Bordeaux (a stunning year and rating):

"What constitutes a great red wine: first, an incredibly dark color, which is an indication of its concentration. Second, amazing fruitiness and ripeness with fat fleshy flavors that are viscous and mouth-filling. And third, the high alcohol content that came from grapes that had achieved perfect maturity."

I felt his description quite meaningful but all the adjectives in the world will not make a wine great! It has to stand on its own merit and the final test is your nose and taste buds.

And a final personal note to all the above. If you do not start with good fruit, you might as well forget the whole experience of wine making.

WINES DESIGNATED "RESERVE"

I feel that term has been overused and abused! I also feel it is used in marketing to propel sales and definitely a higher price.

It can be so named by the bottling winery and merely might mean it was held longer in the oak barrels or perhaps even in its bottle. But for how long? A week?

Not to put it down, as it is definitely an indication that it is perhaps the best of the run, but how much?

Finally, if the wine you are buying does not state it, it does not mean that you have stepped down.

CREATING AND MAINTAINING A SOCIAL WINE CLUB

I brought the idea from California to Ohio, inspired by wine mentors Art Morel and Antonio Gardella. Our wine club is now eight years old and very successful. We are a very compatible and fun loving group. Our largest endeavor, so far, was a trip with spouses to the Central Coast of California and even experienced meeting both mentors and seeing their tiny winery and Art's wine cellar. Next trip to France or Italy?

Over the years, we changed the name from *Nouveau Terrior* to *Vino Versailles*, which was voted on, with a new logo by the members.

We also added a $200 annual dues to shake out people who liked wine but it was not their passion. The annual dues are used for food, which is gourmet class, as we have Michael Deligatta as a member and he is the chef at the Inn at Versailles. We also have a yearly schedule laid out by the president, who has a one-year term.

Different venues are set for each event and it was agreed that since we started as a stag group, that some events per year would include significant others, which are the most important events of the year. Also, with permission of the setting president, a few guests may be invited.

Our sealed group size is sixteen to keep it more personal. New members are interviewed and voted on at a later date. We draw from a thirty mile radius and each event is themed. It began as a loosely-put-together group of wine

The original Vino Versailles meeting at my home in 2009.

lovers, which was led by Todd Dammeyer, who is a second level Sommelier and also Mike Williams who owns, along with his family and wife Carol, the Winery at Versailles, a very successful and entrepreneurial endeavor. Another important member and founder is Michael Deligatta, the very successful chef at the Inn at Versailles.

Typical casting themes might be:

- Wines from the southern hemisphere; wines from France; Washington State; Napa; etc.
- Wines from a special event in your life with the story that goes with it.
- Special items from your wine cellar, with their stories.

Each person brings a bottle and briefly explains its origin, etc. Bread and cheese are on the tables along with a pitcher of water and a dump bucket along with a few appetizers. Each glass is flushed between wines.

This pattern, although small changes do occur, has worked quite well.

🍷 VINO VERSAILLES WINE CLUB BYLAWS
Approved by Group on April 17, 2014

1 Dues will be $200 per year per member. Any member in arrears over twelve months will be dropped from the club. Membership will be sealed at sixteen members.

2 The president will act as the treasurer operating the club on a cash, out-of-pocket, basis for simplicity. A verbal cash report will be given at each event.

3 The president will serve a term of twelve months and will layout four event dates at the beginning of each year. Each president will serve a term by alphabetical order. Anyone refusing to serve will be asked to resign. One event per year will include spouses.

4 Members not attending for twelve months will be asked to resign. New members must be elected by majority vote. It is imperative that any new proposed members have a "deep passion" for wine. New members should NOT be present during the vote.

5 Members may invite a guest at their own cost but should be cleared by the president first. Other wine groups must be invited by the same rules. Outside professional speakers on the subject are encouraged.

6 All events will be held in the Versailles area for simplicity although the president may decide another venue,

including private homes that he chooses. The president may decide a day chairman if he chooses.

7 Each member will bring a themed wine for each event. Mentioning price is optional. In the spirit of the founding of the club it is understood to keep retail price at $25 per bottle or less. The president will decide on a menu for each event. Dump buckets and water will also be provided.

8 A group photo will be taken each year for posterity and a scrapbook.

9 Eight members present will constitute a quorum and at least eight members must RSVP prior to cancellation of a meeting.

🦋 SOCIALLY SPEAKING

When invited to a dinner party, it is almost a must to bring a gift, a bottle of wine or some flowers. If bringing wine, if you give a bottom shelf wine, it is insulting to your hosts and you will look quite cheap in spite of the effort and unappreciative of the invitation. We have always told our family A.B.S.—Always Bring Something, responding to an invitation, and the same goes for a following thank you note.

When receiving the wine, you might ask, "Shall we open it?" If not, we always enjoy writing the guests name and the date on the label, cellaring it, and when opening it, at a later date, recalling the evenings' pleasure.

We prefer not to be overbearing on pairing wine types with the meal. What you really want is just the right wine for the right guest. Never forget, the word *entertaining* is just that. Having your guests happy is paramount.

Sequentially, we always believe white before red; light before heavy; and less alcohol before more.

We do not think it wise to serve a jewel of a wine to an un-appreciating audience. They will never appreciate it, nor remember it. Accordingly, we have never felt guilty with starting with our very best wine and then moving into a lower class wine as the evening moves forward, as long as it is not plonk.

We always figure a half bottle per guest in our planning.

Finally, if you are having a dinner party, make sure the guests are well marinated before you serve dinner. That will drive the amount of food compliments that you will receive.

🦪 TERROIR

Most Americans would run from the term, but it is simply pronounced "ter-wa."

The backbone of any great grape is from the soil it is grown in. That is its terroir. It is simply impossible to copy or replicate, due to the complexity of the earth's crust.

Philosophically, I compare it to two children. One grows up rich, spoiled, and lazy. The other, poor but with lots of tough experiences (stressed). Which one has the most character and strength?

Flat, loamy soil with irrigation, does produce a great yield in terms of grape tonnage; perhaps four tons per acre. Stressed locations (soil) will get only one or two tons per acre. The stressed location will produce fewer grapes per cluster, which means higher quality fruit and enhanced flavors, as roots can go as deep as thirty feet.

I compare it to a farmer who tiles their fields. The biggest reason of course is to drain off excess moisture, but in doing so, it also causes the root system to go deeper and thus discover the nutrients not in the top soil. That is where the taste magic of great grapes is hidden.

Concluding, a good grape starts in a good vineyard with the right soil. Add to that sun exposure, wind speed, and direction, etc.

VALUE

The cardinal rule for any wine purchaser is, "A great wine at an attractive price." It has much to do with the consumer *feel-good* emotion that comes with that purchase.

And, price has nothing to do with the taste. But it has everything to do with the venue, scarcity, publicity, and the amount placed on the market which drives exclusivity. High prices exist because someone is willing to pay them. The cost of production is essentially the same. But, the cost of capital and initial investment does enter into the picture. And tying up capital while the wine is being aged does get expensive. I once read that an investment in a good Napa vineyard will take fourteen years to pencil! That is a lot of tied up capital and it is a game for the very wealthy.

Research has shown that people will consistently rate the taste of an expensive wine higher. In fact, I was in the army with a person who said they had to mark up the price of their champagne higher than normal or it just would not sell. Of course, a retailer will avoid handling inexpensive wines as the profit is just too thin for them to handle. The effort in retailing is somewhat fixed, so I cannot say I would blame them.

At a restaurant, a good way to discover wines is by the glass or cruet (very classy), but you must realize, once you have ordered three glasses, you have paid for the entire bottle. If you enjoy the flavor simply ask for the name. Of course, the taster can be highly influenced by the venue, friends, smells, etc. Might I add, if they do not have a preservation system, it may have been open too long and taste like it was filtered through old coffee grounds.

Another thing to remember about ordering by the glass, is that it is highly profitable for the restaurant as they may get up to five pours from a bottle if the glasses are small. And lower priced restaurants love small glasses.

A much better way to do it, even it you are alone, is to order by the bottle with intention of taking home what is left in the bottle doggy bag style. And it will still be good to drink the next day provided you cork it and refrigerate it overnight. Most states allow Open Take Home and it gives you a chance to reflect on the taste the next day. Is it still the same?

Finally, these economic general comments: The mark-up for a wine store is 1½ times the wholesale cost. For a restaurant, it is two to three times the wholesale cost. And personally speaking, they both deserve it and need it to survive. For example:

Wholesale–$10.00

Retail–$15.00

Restaurant–$20.00 / $30.00

🍂 SOME COMMENTS ON THE ECONOMICS OF WINE

Great European wines are all about nuance, subtlety, and expression. These come from making wines the old fashioned way. That is, labor intense, i.e., picking by hand and long, long barrel aging. These of course, tie up capital and capital is expensive.

Once the conglomerators got into wine and the old *artistes* sold out, the situation drove itself, as the conglomerators had the capital and the marketing prowess, to continue the new trend. And it is now a capital game.

But, capital tied up, also brought on stainless steel tank aging and chaptalization (adding sugar). This brought on *jammy* wines because natural hangtime produces natural sugar and the old world subtlety.

Financially, it is smarter to be *jammy* and higher in alcohol percentage. Fruit forward and high alcohol wines today, drive the market.

Sun drenched fruit and high alcohol overwhelm the taste buds and thus win blind tastings.

This has worked against the French wines, which are much more subtle and terrior (earth) driven. One of the things that drive that, is that there is simply much less sunshine throughout the growing season in Europe.

Wine Experiences

Since beer added to my weight and I watch my weight closely, I finally decided to switch to wine which I did not care for at the time. I started with rosé then went to white and finally to red which would give me headaches, but I had read about the health benefits of red and stuck with it. It led me to Merlot and finally to Cabernet Sauvignon, which is my favorite varietal to this day. My tenacity paid off as I no longer get headaches from Cabernet.

Esther and I decided to do a bike trip in Napa and among the first wines I had there was Chardonnay with a buttery flavor. Foolishly, I thought all Chardonnays were like that. Well, through the years I have had fun checking the honesty of wine shop sales people when I would ask for "a red with the buttery flavor!"

Being the luckiest people in the world and with my business travel, we have had wine in the Loire Valley of France, Tasmania, Israel, Italy, Spain, and New Zealand. Well, I suppose the peak scene may have been at a hacienda event in Spain. Being very hot, I asked for a beer instead of wine. After a few sips, I felt something funny in my mouth. I jumped up and spit out a bee which probably stung the inside of my mouth six times. I switched to a glass of wine!

One night in Napa with World Presidents, we were invited to the old Christian Brothers winery which had been sold and switched to a very impressive home. In the country yard, there was a large swimming pool with the tables around it. There were two opera singers who sang to each other from different sides of the pool. As luck would have it, we were at a table of ten and who was sitting near us but Robert Mondavi! What a treat!

At a dinner party at our home in Versailles one night, we had two couples in for dinner. One of the wives was from Canada and asked if we minded if her brother joined them. We included him and he brought with him three homemade bottles of ice wine which we had not even heard of. They were delicious and sure brought up the sound volume. It was a neat time.

At a World Presidents' event one night, Julia Child was the speaker. She was great and Esther and I had our picture taken with her. It is at the Inn at Versailles in one of the dining rooms to this day.

This is one of the four Alsatian sculptures at the entrances to Versailles, Ohio. The original founders of Versailles were from the Alsace/Lorrain area of France. These were given to the village by Esther and me as a gift to commemorate the 100th founding anniversary of Midmark Corporation. They also signify Versailles' linkage into wine with a winery, wine festival, and French restaurant. Versailles is known as the "Wine Capital of the Miami Valley."

Esther and I with Julia Child in 1995.

As I got deeper into the enjoyment of wine and its gaining popularity, I decided to buy some California vineyard property. Well, I searched a hundred-mile diameter and after a year or so, I found thirty-four acres for sale by an owner right outside of Los Alamos, California, which I could actually afford. It was within site of Route 101 and had some new homes near it. Well, being a little intelligent, I thought, I know nothing of growing wine, so I searched for and found a wine consultant. We had lunch at the Union Hotel there and then went out to view the property. He felt that I would get some flack from the homeowners due to sprayer drift, so I dropped the idea. What is there today? New homes. That should get me the ding-dong award for the year!

In Santa Barbara, there are two special places worthy of mention where we often take guests for a picnic. The first is a winery called Rancho Sisquoc. It is near Los

The Liberty Room at the Inn at Versailles.

Olivos and you find it off Foxen Canyon Road (a very scenic road). Owned by the Flood family since 1952, it has 37,000 acres. They have 150 acres of grapes and the balance is in cattle and farming in general. It is so huge that it seems that airplanes do not even fly over it. It even has its own Catholic chapel. There is a wonderful picnic ground there and it is probably the quietest place we have ever been.

The second place leaves from Los Olivos also, and it is on Figueroa Mountain Road. Go to the top and you will find a wonderful picnic spot with a view that is stunning. It, too, is beautifully quiet.

We moved Midmark to Versailles, Ohio, in about 1980 and we felt it needed a good restaurant. Having traveled all my life, I made notes as I went about restaurant environments that had a good feel to them. Well, Esther and I put the notes together and found a great designer/

decorator and created the Inn at Versailles. It is an Alsatian restaurant with three fireplaces and four rooms plus a nice bar area. It has done quite well. It is French and is well-managed. Our chef is just great! It also has twenty-two sleeping rooms for overnight guests. We are thankful for all of the people who were and are involved. Might I add that it has a great reputation.

In the early 1990s, a neat couple from Pennsylvania purchased a farm near Versailles and created the Winery at Versailles. They were just named Best Winery in Ohio by *OHIO* magazine. They are very successful and with its great wine festival, Versailles is now called the Wine Capital of the Miami Valley. That is pretty neat!

In 2007, Esther and I celebrated our fiftieth wedding anniversary and we invited about 200 guests. Always looking ahead, I had begun collecting above average wines for the celebration in our cellar for ten years. At the event, Esther insisted that we keep full bottles on all tables. I am sad to report that few of the people truly appreciated the wine, so I felt I had just given away my best child. So much for that.

At a very foxy wine dinner at the Santa Barbara club, one day we were asked to explain any wine experiences we had recently. I was so stunned when one gentleman reported that he was shipping one-hundred thousand dollars of Bordeaux to London for a Christie's auction in the morning. I never felt so under-classed in my life!

I had always wanted to be part of the wine industry and knowing nothing about wine making, I thought I could perhaps invest in a winery and have the fun of feeling included. I had two experiences: one in California and one in the midwest, both being new wineries. Well, starting any new business is always risky. So, I approached both at different times and asked the owners if they might be interested in having a silent partner. Both declined, which told me that it was a good business to be in.

Esther and I were traveling with a Jewish group in the Middle East and we had come into Jerusalem from Jordan. We were staying at the King David Hotel and there was a dinner that night with some local dignitaries. During the dinner, someone from the hotel walked over to us and gave us a fax informing us that our second grandson, Christian Klamar, had been born. I mentioned it, the men jumped up, put a wine glass on their heads, clapped, and exclaimed *mazel tov*! It was just too cute and they never dropped a glass.

COMPAÑEROS WINERY

This is quite an unusual story which starts with a relationship that I stumbled into with a gentleman by the name of Antonio Gardella. Quite a nice gentleman, he was the maître d' at a restaurant named Piatti (Ristorante Piatti) in Santa Barbara. He went on to become one of the sales people of the Henry Wine Group. A graduate of the University of California, he won many wine sales awards and now teaches wine at Santa Barbara City College.

In any event, we began having him over for dinner and he always brought wines from the Compañeros Winery: Syrahs, Pinot Noirs, or Cabernet Sauvignons. He introduced me to a friend of his, Dr. Art Morel and his lovely wife Charice. We later found out that Morel's property actually touched ours in our rear yards and they had a carriage building on it. He also had purchased a redwood wine vat from Graystone Winey, disassembled it, and re-assembled it when he built his home to be his wine cellar. It has a capacity of 5,100 gallons and it is quite a jewel. They actually had twenty people in it at one time, just to see how many it could hold.

Well, with their passion for wine, they met Sid Ackert who had an old horse shed on a creek. The three also knew a gentleman by the name of Luis Goena and they put together a winery in the shed, buying the best grapes that they could in the valley. This was in 1985 and they agreed to make wine only as a hobby but never selling it. They went on to win hundreds of gold medals over the years and raised more than one hundred thousand dollars for charities. They had so much fun doing it!

I would join them on a Saturday morning and would wash bottles and help them when they bottled. It was great fun and the four were just wonderful to work with.

The four original Compañeros and the Compañeros Winery logo.

Compañeros
SANTA BARBARA, CALIFORNIA

Unfortunately, in 2009, there was a tragic fire called Jesusita which swept the valley and took not only Sid's home but also the winery with it. It was quite sad, and they lost eight barrels of finished wine, forty cases of bottles, plus corks, etc. And needless to say, they were quite lost without their passion and hobby.

Well, Art Morel suggested more than once that they restart a smaller winery in the lower level of his carriage house. In 2012, they actually did and reignited their first love. Art's wife, Charice, was able to keep her art studio on the first level so it is quite a poetic location. She is the artist who graciously painted the cover for this book. We thank her very much!

COMPAÑEROS: A QUARTER OF A CENTURY MAKING HOME WINE TOGETHER

"Compañeros means *buddies* and it is the name of a home winery located in the foothills of Santa Barbara, California. In 1985, Adam Tolmach needed help to pick his first vintage at the Ojai Vineyard. Four friends helped picked Adam's Zinfandel grapes from sunrise to sunset. Adam then declared his fermenting bins full. "If you want to pick some Zinfandel grapes for yourself, go right ahead." We looked at each other and headed back to the vineyard, snipping enough dark, ripe fruit to make one barrel. Our first effort led us to make another barrel in 1986, and we turned an old abandoned, redwood horse stable into a winery. We made about twelve barrels of wine each year for nearly twenty-five years. We made Pinot Noir, Syrah, Petite Sirah, Cabernet Franc, Cabernet Sauvignon, Roussanne, Viognier, Malbec, Sauvignon Blanc, Zinfadel, Merlot, and Nebbiolo from local vineyards including Julia's,

The three remaining Compañeros, 2016.

Bien Nacido, Ashley's, Sierra Madre, Sweeney, Hilltop, Lafond, Buttonwood, Rancho Sisquoc, Roll Ranch, Zaca Mesa, Thompson, Stolpman, and Honea. Compañeros Winery was hosted by owner Sid Ackert, who was joined by Luis Goena, Dr. Art Morel, and Antonio Gardella. Over the years the four friends earned one hundred gold medals, including Best Red Wine at the Orange County Fair, Santa Barbara Fair, and California State Fair for their 2001 Pinot Noir. The fine quality of their wines became legendary and charities asked for donations of wine, which fetched $1,000 to $4,000 a case at auctions. They raised scores of thousands of dollars for the Boys Club, Rotary, Santa Barbara Chamber Orchestra, Braille Institute, Sansum Diabetes Foundation, and many others. Unfortunately, in 2009, the Jesusita Fire burned the winery and Sid's home to ashes. Unable to find a place to continue, the Compañeros remain great friends and have fond memories of the years getting purple fermenting the delicious local Santa Barbara County wine grapes. They never sold a bottle; their wines have been enjoyed by friends and family. Such is the stuff of legends in the local wine world." *

❧ CHIPPED WINE GLASSES

In 1985, we were in Bucharest, Romania, while it was still communistic and had a luncheon while their symphony performed for us. They were quite good.

The wine glasses we had were crystal and very beautiful but we noticed the edges of them were chipped. Half-

*From the *Santa Barbara News Press.*

way through the performance, Esther's chair broke and she followed the waiter out to get a replacement. She noted in the storage room that it was full of broken chairs. She did get a replacement that worked.

At that point, we felt that the communist system was failing and we were quite correct!

❧ A MOST WONDERFUL GLASS OF WINE

Back in the late 80s, Esther and I had traveled on the Danube from Vienna to the Black Sea with lots of side trips. This was when the Iron Curtain was still up. We had started in East Berlin and I remember having dinner and paying with U.S. dollars, receiving East German marks in change, and then going up one floor for an after-dinner drink. I paid for the drinks with East German marks and they would not take them. They wanted U.S. dollars.

It was an interesting trip and sometimes scary with machine guns pointed at the river. We were never allowed to leave the boat with our passports. They held them until our return.

Well, then in the early 90s after the Wall came down, I went on two trips as a guest of *Chief Executive* magazine. The idea was to showcase the free enterprise system in Eastern Europe and Russia. It was a very interesting experience as people were so dirt poor. They were actually afraid of the free enterprise system as many of them had spent their entire lives under the socialist system.

At that time we had a hospital division and sold operating tables, stretchers, etc. We felt we needed operating room lights to complete our offering. Operating lamps are quite different. They must be cool lighting as once the incision is made, you must be very careful to keep it from drying up.

We learned of a company in Lodz, Poland, who made them for the eastern block countries. For some reason on my second trip there, Esther was with me. We flew into Warsaw which had been carpet bombed by Germany in World War II and they were doing their best to rebuild it and the Soviets had put up some ugly buildings. Surprisingly, Marriott had a new hotel there.

I noticed they had a casino on the seventh floor and I love to throw the dice. We hired a driver/interpreter who was quite young and not very experienced in driving. We were on a two-lane highway and after a near second head-on crash I said, "If you don't slow down, I am not paying you!" It worked. It was a two-hour drive.

Poland is very fertile and flat. You could roll a dime to Moscow it seemed. Most farms had gone collective with the buildings destroyed and the operators living in small villages. There was little mechanized equipment and the wives were in the fields with hoes, wearing their babushkas with their hose rolled down to their ankles. I noticed that at the few remaining farms, there were alters at the end of the lane. Poland is very Catholic. I asked the driver about the alters and he said the saying, "First one through the rosary, first one to the dance" still held.

We did visit the factory and returned to the Marriott that evening. I said to Esther, I am going to have a glass of wine and do some gambling. She said she was tired and was going up to the room to wash her hair.

I got my glass of wine and decided, in spite of it being a poor odds game, I would play Roulette. At the time, the exchange was 1,700 zlotys per dollar. I gave them $100 and I got 170,000 zlotys...lots of chips. I sipped my wine slowly as I take gambling seriously. Well, I got down to 1,700 zlotys which was $1 and suddenly I came back, and fast! By my count, I had 1,190,000 zlotys. I also noticed as my chips piled up, several very attractive girls walked around the table. My luck faded as quickly as it had arrived and I declared cash out. You can't believe how poor those people were and mothers would do anything to get enough money to buy milk for their infants. I said "cash out," went to the cashier, and put $700 into my billfold.

I began to walk to the elevators and several said that they would like to go to my room with me. I frankly said, "I am a married man." They persisted and I said, "My wife is in our room!" They said "She won't care." And I replied "You don't know my wife!"

We ended up not buying the company but it was a wonderful glass of wine.

🍷 LIMA, PERU

We were traveling with World Presidents in Lima, Peru, in 1990, and we got paired off with two other couples for

dinner. The men found that they had in common the love of wine. We had just finished our cistern wine cellar and I proudly mentioned that we could hold up to 500 bottles. Well, the gentleman from Iowa stated that his would hold 1,000 bottles and finally the man from Palm Springs mentioned that he stores 10,000 bottles! These two were solid successes and had no reason to brag. It sure put me in my place!

Fifty years ago my parents liked to vacation in New Orleans. Esther and I were newly married, so they asked us to join them. (I think they wanted me for a driver.) One night, my father said the dinner was on him so he took us to Antoine's which is a very famous and upscale restaurant in the French Quarter. Following dinner, our waiter asked if we would like to see their wine cellar and I accepted. It was like going to Transylvania, with many racks, dust, and spider webs. It wasn't unsanitary, they were just aging wine that long and in that volume. A beer drinker at that time, I would love to repeat that today after devel-

oping my love of wine. Also, I was too young and dumb to even think of tipping the man. I am sure he thought I was cheap but I was just that ignorant.

FAVORITE WINE SAYINGS

- It is only the first bottle of wine that is expensive.
- Money spent in caring for good wine is well spent.
- Life is too short to drink bad wine.
- Wine improves with age; the older I get, the more I like it.
- Friends and wine should both be old.
- Never think of leaving your wine to your heirs. Drink them yourself and let the heirs have the money.
- Water separates the people of the world but wine unites them.
- Selfishness is an emotion unknown to wine lovers.
- Where there is wine, sorrow and worry take wing.
- Wine was created from the beginning to make people joyful, not to make them drunk.

- The juice of the grape is the liquid quintessence of concentrated sunbeams.
- A meal without wine is like a day without sunshine.
- A meal without wine is called breakfast.
- As I age, I find I need glasses, hopefully full of good wine.
- Everyone has to believe in something, so I believe I shall have another glass of wine.
- Diogenes was asked what wine he liked the best and he answered "somebody elses."
- Open the bottle and allow it to breathe. If it does not look like it is, give it mouth to mouth resuscitation.

WINE THOUGHTS

Believe in something or you will fall for anything. Find your favorite varietal and make yourself a specialist in it. Focus, focus, focus! Learn everything you can about that varietal that you can.

In terms of making yourself a wine devotee, you must first develop your sensory perception, from nose to palate, and then on to mental perception.

Wine is not made to be a stand alone drink. It always needs food with it to balance it out. Something as simple as cheese or crackers will suffice and they always pair well. They will cancel out other flavors, especially strong ones.

In terms of calories, a glass of wine equals a medium apple or a slice of bread. One glass equals 120 calories.

Red wine is rich in a flavonoid called "resveratrol". It is a super potent antioxidant also found in blueberries.

That is the reason that two glasses of red wine are recommended for your daily health.

Wines are like people. The older they get, the stronger their character. But, like the best people, that character melds into wisdom and softness as they age.

From a friend and wine mentor, Antonio Gardella, on good wine: "An eighteen-year-old can look great, but a fifty-year-old is more interesting, as they have simply been around longer."

The best glass of white wine is the first, but the best glass of red wine is the last.

If you find a wine you really like at a party or restaurant, take a photo of the label for retention.

Finally, wine makes me more of who I truly am.

A few resource websites

eRobertParker.com (wine advocate)
winespectator.com
wineberserkers.com
winebusiness.com
winebusinessmonthly.com
winesearcher.com (a map of easy ways to locate and price wines)

2

Wines
and Locations

Bordeaux, France

🍇 BORDEAUX

Bordeaux is not a separate wine varietal at all but a region of France with a long legacy of producing excellent wines. Its reputation is legendary, although certain years in terms of quality are more important than others due to weather swings.

It is a combination (or meritage) of Cabernet Sauvignon, Merlot, Cabernet Franc, Petit Verdot, and Malbec. It is also called Claret but basically it is Cabernet Sauvignon.

The reason that French winemakers are less focused on making wines from just one grape than those in the southern hemisphere and elsewhere, is partly because they believe that climate and soil are more important than the fruit on the vines.

Unlike California wines, with their power, early finish and higher alcohol, Bordeaux, though less attractive in its youth, tends to be more subtle. It develops its complexity over time, which is always on its side (it can age for decades). Naturally, storage temperature becomes very important. Good ones have a nice finesse about them, even with their lower alcohol content.

Their ultimate aroma can have a cedary, cigar box odor. Though they can be low in alcohol, thin bodied and still have subtle tannins, they are legendary versus California wines with their more aggressiveness, alcohol content, and heaviness.

The finish in a good Bordeaux wine is worthy of mention also.

🐚 BRANDY

Simply stated, brandy is a twice distilled spirit, made from a wine base to concentrate the flavor, color, and alcohol percentage. Aged at least two years in French oak barrels and it usually is between thirty-five percent and sixty percent alcohol. Some may have coloring added to imitate aging.

In the after dinner category, it is also used as a deglazing liquid for sauces and meats. It does tend to intensify the flavor.

Most popular brands are Cognac, Armagnac, and others which are produced in those areas of France.

🐚 BURGUNDY

Burgundy is actually a tiny wine region of France, at the northern limit of the great wine growing region. Its wines, even at a high price, can come in uneven quality. This is due to the wide weather swings that they have there. Its reds are essentially Pinot Noir and its whites are Chardonnay.

🐚 CABERNET FRANC

Although rarely seen alone, it is a minor red grape and considered by many to be Cabernet Sauvignon's best friend, but also its poor cousin.

Although compared to the Cabernet Sauvignon varietal, it does lack weight and tannin. It has a starring role in the production of France's famous Bordeaux blend and it is very popular in the Loire Valley of France.

🍇 CABERNET SAUVIGNON

Cabernet Sauvignon is the gold standard and always will be. It has layers of flavors, tends to be tannic in its youth to mature slowly and to live long. It is the classiest and most popular of all wines.

Since Cabernet Sauvignon's spiritual home is Bordeaux, this superb and noble grape is largely responsible for the great clarets of Bordeaux. It also makes up the core of most fine wine auctions.

It seems to grow quite well in the Napa Valley and the Paso Robles area of California has done well with it also. Might I add that Washington State is beginning to place some good Cabernet wines as well.

At the end of the day, after being into wines for twenty-five years, this is without a doubt, my very favorite and always will be.

🍇 CHABLIS

Coming from the Burgundy region of France and the Chardonnay grape, this is a wonderful white wine that goes well with seafood. At least once in your life, pair it with raw oysters. They feel like they belong together.

It has a unique streak of acidity, reminding one of flint or wet stone. That flavor comes from chalky limestone soil, supposedly created millions of years ago by marine organisms.

One of the latest buzz words in the wine industry is *minerality*, which is described as the meeting point of wet and dry, verses adjectives such as fruity, oaky, spicy, and herbal. A good example of it is Mosel Rieslings, although not quite the same.

❧ CHAMPAGNE

Champagne is a region of France ninety miles from Paris. One of the coolest winemaking regions in the world, it is alone in its distinction.

In a sense, Champagne is a state of mind and usually a cause for celebration.

Most Champagnes are a blend of Chardonnay, Pinot Noir, and Pinot Meunier. However, Pink Rose Champagne is considered the crème de la crème of all Champagnes. The blends go from eighty percent Chardonnay and twenty percent Pinot Noir or the opposite.

Making Champagne involves a second fermentation which creates the bubbles (carbon dioxide) or pressure. The pressure is seventy-five pounds per square inch or three times the pressure of a car tire. It is necessary to use thicker glass for the bottles for that reason and a deep punt in the bottom for additional strength. Brut is a term used for the most popular dry Champagne.

Champagne Temperature—Champagne or sparkling wines must always be served much colder than still wines because sparkling wines are generally high in acid. High acid wines are particularly unpleasant to drink warm. Plus, the cold preserves the bubbles and thus the longer the sparkle will hold. The inverse is true as well; warm

Champagne will taste flat, which is exactly what a Champagne drinker does not want.

🍷 CHARDONNAY

Chardonnay is the gold standard of all whites and the heaviest. It is the only white that can be cellared for long periods and the white that must be aged in oak.

In my earliest wine experiences, I had a Chardonnay that actually had a buttery flavor. That is possible but it only happened to me once.

🍷 CHENIN BLANC

A native of Franc's Loire Valley, it is relatively high in acid and is France's answer to German Riesling. In some ways, it could be the world's most noble and yet discredited grape. It is extremely versatile and can be produced in a wide range of styles from bone dry to rather sweet. It will never be as popular as Chardonnay or as respected as Riesling. Rarely commanding a high price, it is thus a good value.

🍷 GAMAY

Coming exclusively from the Beaujolais area of France and many times marketed under the Beaujolais label, it is truly a French wine. Outside of France, though, it is virtually non-existent.

Of all the reds, Gamay is actually the simplest, with very little tannin. It has a distinctive fruity flavor. Always consumed when cool, it is a happy wine and enjoyed by many.

This quote is from *The Emperor of Wine* book, "Beaujolais is a young girl. Burgundy is a women of thirty."

GRENACHE

Its spiritual home is in the Rhone Valley. It is used quite often in blending there.

Its characteristics are high alcohol and affordability. It tends to be dry and its bouquet is unremarkable. It has low acidity and tannins.

It is moderately colored and goes to brown quickly.

ICE WINE

Germany is a top producer of Ice Wine but Canada is actually the largest producer in the world. In fact, at a dinner party one evening, several Canadians joined us and brought a bottle that they had produced themselves. It was wonderful!

Picked at night while frozen solid, bunches of grapes come in as hard as marbles and must be picked one by one. It can be produced in any varietal.

The frozen grapes are left with the skin on, which makes it very tender. It is a concentrated flavor, balanced by its high sugar and acidity.

Meant to be sipped like Port, it is quite sweet.

Because the amount of labor is multiplied, it is usually sold in 0.375 MM bottles.

MALBEC

It is Argentina! Surprisingly thin-skinned, it is well suited to the hot, high altitudes of the above. With dense, rich chewy tannins, and lively acidity, it is best described as a meatier version of Merlot. Flavors are straightforward with hints of spices and red berries.

MERLOT

When I first switched from white to red wines, Merlot was my first choice and I did enjoy it.

It is an enjoyable wine and is a great starter wine as people move into reds. It is quite soft but it is not nuanced like Cabernet. It is just not challenging in terms of breadth of flavor (not interesting).

Recent Merlot sales have faded as many people have moved on to Malbec and Syrah.

NEBBIOLO

Almost a hard grape to describe with love, it is one of the most renowned grapes of Italy, notable the Piedmont region. In the minds of Italians, Nebbiolo holds a place equal to Cabernet Sauvignon in France.

With a very distinctive flavor, it might be impossible to compare it with any other wine. It is high in acidity and tannin, although somewhat more forgiving when young.

As it ages, it gets a burnt and tarry flavor which does make an impression.

PINOT GRIS

It is a crisp, fresh white wine and rather hard to describe. Depending on where it is grown, the taste and even the color can be different.

It can be from Italy, Germany, Oregon or even California and each with its own personality.

PINOT NOIR

Pinot Noir is a light wine, low in tannins, which I would put in the Merlot category of red wine.

It thrives in cooler climates such as Oregon's Willamette Valley or Northern California. It was first planted in Oregon in the 1960s.

It is the principal grape used in Burgundy wines. Burgundy is actually a very quiet area of France and not a varietal at all. Soft and smooth as velvet, would be my description of it.

PORT

All Port comes from the Douro Valley of Portugal. The valley is best described as tough, hot, and also cold. The soil, not rich in the least, is a tough place for any vine to grow. The varietals that grow there are over eighty types which are co-mingled. The terrain obviously makes the grapes small and rich in flavor as a result. Surprisingly, some of the grapes are still foot treadled in the vat by people without shoes.

The beginning port is a blend of the above. After fermenting only two to three days, it is given a dose of neutral spirits, which kills the yeast in the wine. The ratio used is one part of spirits to four parts of wine. This is called fortification.

The types of Port are:

Ruby—This is the basic type and also least expensive. It is aged two to three years from darker fuller grapes. Best described as sweet and light.

Douro Valley, Portugal.

Late Bottled Vintage—Aged in wood and bottled four to six years after vintage.

Tawny—A single vintage, aged in wood casks for ten years or more for the best ones. It is relaxed and earthy, pale in color, mellow and nutty, with a woody, dried fruit flavor. It is thought that twenty years is the perfect age for a Tawny.

Colheita—A single vintage Tawny too, but picked in a single vintage, then placed in casks for a minimum of ten-plus years before bottling. Colheita constitutes only one percent of all Ports produced (and is my favorite).

Vintage—This is the cream of the milk bottle. Vintage Port must be collectively declared together by all the grape producers and happens only a few times per decade. It is aged in wood two years before bottling, and then held for ten to fifteen years before release. It is highly expensive and collectible and has a good concentration of consumers in London. It is like a song; a symphony.

On a concluding comment, it is one of the few wines that can be safely held for over one hundred years and the ultimate flavor is the one with a nutty finish. It pairs very well with Stilton and Blue Cheeses and can be held for up to a week after opening if refrigerated. Our favorite cheese is buttermilk blue from Wisconsin. It is very creamy and has good longevity and is also hard to find.

Port is meant to be consumed after a meal in small amounts due to its twenty percent alcohol level.

Here is another personal note. I was extremely fortunate as the first bottle of Port that I ever purchased was one with a nutty flavor. I went back for another and the vendor could only say it was gone, which also assumes how rare the nutty flavor truly is!

🐌 RHONE WINES

They are hard to describe due to their wide geography. The Rhone River begins high in the Alps and then flows through France finally dumping into the Mediterranean near Marseille. It is divided into two parts, the north and the south, both being notable for different varietals. There are at least twenty-three varietals with the main classic red grape being Syrah, but Grenache is important too, mainly used in blending. The main white is Viognier.

The Rhone Wines can be quite charming, a combination of warm climate and blending. As in many French wines, the combination of grapes to be found in Côtes du Rhône is far, far more then the sum of its parts.

The most popular labels of Côtes du Rhône can be staple wines in cafes in France, America, or anywhere. They might come from north or south. They are not in a league with Bordeaux but they are a good table wine which is popular and well-priced.

We always enjoy them and are never disappointed.

RIESLING

Primarily from Germany's Rhine and Mosel regions, this is a wine with a remarkable balance of acidity and fruit. It also has an almost beguiling aroma of minerals.

It is expensive to produce there, as the steep hillsides on which it grows call for a picked-by-hand harvest.

It is generally lower in alcohol than reds and will be between seven and ten percent.

It has great agreeability and can outlast almost any other wine in the world.

From the United States, New York's Finger Lakes Region is a dynamic wine area. Riesling is their signature varietal and it is quite good, as well.

SANGIOVESE

A red grape from Italy, Sangiovese is the primary grape used in Red Chianti and in every major traditional Italian wine. It is considered one of the greatest grapes of Italy. Sangiovese seems built for food. It is much more supple and less tannic than Cabernet Sauvignon. It has a good deal of acidity that clears your palate and is light on bouquet. Red Italian Chianti is medium bodied and rarely dark in color.

SAUTERNES

Sauternes is made from Sémillon, Sauvignon Blanc, and Muscadelle grapes in the Sauternais region of Bordeaux. It is a sweet wine, served before or after a meal.

The most beguiling of all them is the Premier Cru from Chateau d'Yquem (pronounced "E-Come"). It is a wine affected with Botrytis cinerea (noble rot) which must be hand harvested and it requires a whole vine just to make one glass. Therefore, it is very expensive.

🍇 SAUVIGNON BLANC

A noble grape along with Chardonnay and Riesling, it is not an outstanding varietal but solid nevertheless.

Sauvignon Blanc is just the opposite of Chardonnay with its buttery roundness and softness. Sauvignon Blanc is taut, herbal, and high in acid. Being very kind, I would say grassy and herbaceous. It finds its home in Bordeaux, The Loire Valley, California, New Zealand, South Africa, and other places around the world, as well.

🍇 SHERRY

Sherry, dating back to the Romans, is a fortified wine and deliberately oxidized. It is sold at seventeen percent and was once called sack. It is also sold under the name Cream Sherry, which is the same.

It is a pleasant wine which I would put in the Aperitif category. But it can also be served during an entire meal or at the end of a meal much like Port. It is made exclu-

sively in Andalusia, which is in southern Spain. Sherry is simply a fortified, sweetened wine. Although used mostly as an Aperitif, it should always be served with toasted almonds. It is also quite popular in the making of turtle soup.

🍷 SYRAH

One of the noblest of red grapes, it is also known as a Shiraz in Australia. A lead grape in Northern Rhone Wines, the Rhone Valley of France is its spiritual home. It has subtle hints of spices in its flavor. Although it was late in coming to California in the late 1980s, they do produce some good Syrah wines. When young, it tends to produce more power than finesse. It is a heavy wine.

🍷 VIOGNIER

It is pronounced Vee-en-eh. It is what I would call an afternoon wine. It is a very pleasant white on the lighter side, not competing at all with Chardonnay. Chardonnay is the type of wine you would serve at a lengthy event or dinner.

Viognier is fruit forward without being overwhelming in the fruit direction. Not dry in any way, it has a wonderful suggestion of peach, yet very subtle in that direction. Low in acid, it has a nice conversation feel to it with a nice finish. It can be consumed without food and is one of our favorites.

Originally from the Rhone Valley of France, it has been adopted by some wineries in America and other countries as well. A sister wine to it would be Silvaner.

If you are a red drinker and want a good transitional or bridge wine to white, it is perfect for that.

Finally, I have always felt that the name frightens people away as they have a problem pronouncing it and at first glance think *vinegar*.

🐌 ZINFANDEL

Although its origins are traced back to Croatia, California is where it is centered worldwide and had been for 200 years. It is the oldest vine in California and is number two there in acreage. It is a dry, flexible wine and comes in both red and white.

American Wines

American wines are definitely popular in America. Almost three quarters of wine consumed in America is grown and produced there. America has tremendous advantages in addition to being a huge market. Things like the price of American oak barrels and the average price per land in most places, less freight and import duty, do add up to good value. And everyone, everywhere likes good value.

In addition, the fruit grown in America has proven to create good wines crafted by skilled people.

Finally, as I have said about many things, when a price point and a quality product agree, a sale happens easily.

❧ CALIFORNIA WINES

On May 24, 1976, at a blind tasting in France, something happened that shook the entire world! Two wines from California were chosen above the Grand Cru's of France. That was an epic moment and things have never been the same since.

Although the question remains, "Would the California Cabernets, though massive and powerful, stand the test of time as well as the French Bordeaux?" California wines do tend to be more fruit forward and categorically more of a drink-now wine, but I personally am very comfortable with the ten-year storage limit I have placed on them.

That being said, I do not know of a wine that cannot be grown successfully in California. They are so gifted in terms of level weather, sun, and varied terriors. They have become a major world power and will remain so due to the growth of this great entrepreneurial and fun industry. It has been accompanied by some very good education at California schools such as the University of California at Davis, etc., but they just seem to be getting better.

The state of California produces ninety percent of all the wines in America. Ironically, the Central Valley is 450 miles long and produces sixty percent of the fruit of that state. Although all we hear is Napa, Napa, Napa, Paso Robles and Sonoma produce some great wines also and at a much more dear price. Many state locations are quite successful.

The state is gifted with 840 miles of Pacific Coast which creates a haven for growing good grapes.

NEW YORK WINES

New York ranks third in grape production by volume in the U.S. California and Washington are first and second. Major varietals include Reisling, Sauvignon Blanc, Chardonnay, Pinot Noir, Cabernet Sauvignon, and various sparking type wines. Major wine areas are: Lake Erie, Finger Lakes, Hudson River Valley, and Eastern Long Island.

OHIO WINES

As a native Ohioan, I must mention to you that Versailles, the village we live in, is called the "Wine Capital of the Miami Valley." Also, might I add that *OHIO* magazine just named the Winery at Versailles the best winery in Ohio.

First planted in 1823, by 1860, Ohio produced more wine than any other state. Many varietals are grown in the state. It is in the top ten wine producers in America.

OREGON WINES

A state worthy of mentioning is Oregon. Wineries there are generally small and decentralized with most being located in the valley between the Cascade Mountains, notably the Willamette Valley. Their northern latitude allows long hours of summer sunshine.

The cooler climate grape varieties thrive there which include Pinto Gris, Riesling, and Chardonnay, but the most popular by far are their Pinot Noirs.

Luckily, with my brother having a vineyard there, he has been most kind in sending us cases of both Pinot Noir and Pinot Gris.

🐚 WASHINGTON STATE WINES

The Columbia Valley which produces the bulk of all vineyard areas within the state, lies in the Columbia River Plateau. In terms of latitude, it matches the French regions of Bordeaux and Burgundy. Much cooler than the Napa Valley of California, it allows red varietals to ripen slower and develop full and complex flavors.

The soil there is volcanic (schist) and of the sandy loam type, which does offer good drainage but very poor nutrients. This is ideal for the root system's deep search for nutrients. Also, the northern latitude allows additional hours of sunshine during the critical fruit producing summer. Rain is inhibited by the Cascade Range which has forced irrigation systems that allow the growth of really good fruit.

The Yakima Valley is a good area also, but on a much smaller scale. Grapes grown there are Cabernet Sauvignon, Merlot, Chardonnay, Riesling, Syrah, and Pinot Gris. All very fruit forward and classy as well. Washington state is second to California in the U.S. in terms of wine production.

World Wines

ARGENTINE WINES

Argentina is the fifth largest producer of wine in the world. It is also the largest exporter in South America. The Malbec varietal is responsible for most of Argentina's best known wines. The major wine regions are in the western part of the country which is dominated by the Andes Mountains. Its high altitude region is favored by ample water from the melting snows of the Andes.

AUSTRALIAN WINES

Australian wines have been produced in Australia since 1788 and were introduced by the British. It is the world's seventh largest producer and is the fourth largest exporter. It is produced in every state and in every style of wine. Typically, they produce Shiraz, Cabernet Sauvignon, Merlot, Pinot Noir, Riesling, Sauvignon

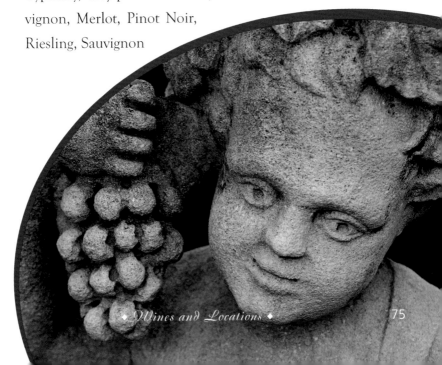

Blanc, and Viognier. It is economically priced and that drives their export success.

CANADIAN WINES

Canadian wine is primarily produced in Southern British Columbia and Southern Ontario. Canadian wines have a less than fifty percent market share in Canada, making it one of the few wine producing countries where the domestic producers do not hold a dominant share. Ice wine is the most recognized product on an international basis.

CHILEAN WINES

Wines grown in Chile date back to the sixteenth century and their plants were brought here from Spain. Chile is the world's ninth largest producer and the fifth largest exporter. Their red wines are Cabernet Sauvignon, Merlot, and Carmenere with the single largest category being Cabernet. They tend to be full flavored, ripe, and fruity. Their reds seem better than the whites. Their white wines are Sauvignon Blanc and Chardonnay.

&. FRENCH WINES

This is a very large subject; too large to cover in any detail in this abridged book. Looking at France's wine history, one must consider that wine has been made here aggressively since before the Roman invasion of Gaul. You have to respect that depth of experience.

Its major region is, of course, Bordeaux which is also the closest to the ocean, looking at the different regions. Bordeaux stands out above all others in every way. The blended Bordeaux wines are the most aristocratic and they have great longevity and are also highly collectible and sought after. Notable sub-regions are Medoc, Pauillac, Saint-Emilion, Pomerol, etc. In terms of area profoundness, Bordeaux is followed by Burgundy, Champagne, The Loire Valley, and the huge Rhone River Valley. That valley is termed "Côtes du Rhône." With their huge variety of blends, they make quite good table wines.

Personally, in studying France, I feel perhaps due to its long history, winemaking in France is overly controlled by the government and thus inhibits entrepreneurship.

Tuscany, Italy.

America and other younger countries, have less rules and thus more robust growth in their wine industries.

🍇 ITALIAN WINES

Wines in Italy are quite good and were actually produced before the Romans started their own vineyards. Italy produces twenty percent of the global production and is second only to France.

Their wines are grown in every region of the country with Tuscany being the center of their wine culture. The climate of Italy imitates North Africa in the south and Switzerland in the north. The red grape Sangiovese is the most important varietal in Italy. Chianti is their most famous wine. Chaptalization (adding sugar) is not permitted in Italy.

🔊 NEW ZEALAND WINES

Wines were first planted in New Zealand in 1819 but somewhat unnoticed until the mid 1980s. They suddenly sprung to life and their wine industry is thriving today. It is also a great and beautiful country to visit and the people there are quite nice. Wineries are located in many regions of the country. Their Sauvignon Blanc wines are quite profound and dominant.

🔊 SOUTH AFRICAN WINES

The wine history in South Africa goes back to 1659 and the production is centered near Cape Town. They did not become an exporter until the late 1980s and 1990s. Chenin Blanc is their most planted grape and is the most popular. Thus, it is the most reasonable in price. Recently however, they have been concentrating on Cabernet Franc and Cabernet Sauvignon.

🔊 SPANISH WINES

Spain is the third largest wine producer in the world. It follows France which is number one and then Italy. It has the most land dedicated to grapes, but that is offset by poor soil and thus wide-row spacing. Among the wine region their La Rioja is the most renowned. It is in North Central Spain. The main red wines are Tempranillo and Grenache. The main white wines would be Airen, Macabeo, and Palomino.

3

Cooking
and Recipes

🍷 COOKING

Although this is not a cookbook, and I am not a professional chef, wine and food do pair and always will. It can be great fun with a near perfect result. It is part of entertaining whether doing it alone or sharing the dish with someone. But, as I see it, you *do* need a glass of wine next to the stove as part of the enjoyment. Wine and cooking have been paired in Europe for centuries.

To me, moisture is the quintessence of any good dish. Once you have lost it, you have lost the dish. And always remember, you cannot un-cook anything!

I have included a few of our favorite recipes, some with wine and some without. Several have been given to us, yet others came from a variety of magazines and papers we

read. I have tried to focus on dishes which are simple to prepare without too much effort. And many can be kept as leftovers, as often times they are best when they sit overnight and are reheated. On the second nights, we add angel hair pasta to them to change the dish somewhat.

One cardinal rule is to cook with wine if at all possible. And with recipes that call for water, you might try substituting one-half wine with one-half water. Wine gives it that special caché. One thing to note here is that with alcohol boiling at 174 degrees Fahrenheit and water at 212 degrees Fahrenheit, cooking it down enhances the flavor. Our rule is to reduce, reduce, reduce, as it does magnify the flavors.

Worthy of mention is that if you start with plonk wine, you will only enhance that flavor. You don't need to

use your top shelf wine, but please do not use the bottom shelf either. Dry is the key word in cooking with wines. With whites, we recommend Savignon Blanc or Pinot Grigio; with reds, Pinot Noir or Zinfandel.

Good pick-ups in any dish are bacon in small amounts, onions, nuts, garlic in small amounts, and sweet tiny red tomatoes. Also, real butter is a key ingredient. Of course, olive oil and balsamic vinegar are a given, as are salt and pepper. In some situations, thinly sliced orange or lemon slices can give anything a zesty flavor. The thing that always concerns me is that any one of them can overpower any dish. Your dinner should be a symphony; flavors should be integrated, like a good wine.

With a heavily herbed dish, you want to be concerned about the same thing. If that happens, you may want to add a dash of Vermouth to soften it a bit.

Mushrooms always remind me of Merlot wine. They are a nice companion to almost anything.

Although cooking together can be fun as it is a neat end of the day exercise, it is as close to divorce as Esther and I get. No kitchen is big enough for two people, especially working at the same counter. Two cutting boards are a necessity. It works best when I'm outside grilling while she is making the salad and veggies. Our favorite night to cook is Sunday after reading the *New York Times*.

A personal note from this amateur chef: I always feel that microwaves have their place, but it seems they congeal what is placed in them, versus when heating with a conventional oven. Also, I am a real fan of cast iron for cooking. Cast iron pans seem to distribute the heat more evenly and certainly retain the heat when serving the food from them. Of course, warm plates are a given.

Finally, I cannot emphasize freshness enough. This statement covers everything from fish to radishes. It is one of the reasons for the success of farmers markets and buying fish on the docks. Like the grape, once it leaves the vine, you begin to lose moisture which translates to freshness. So, fresh, fresh, fresh!

Seventy percent of the fish consumed in the U.S. is in restaurants. What you want to be concerned about is that ninety percent of the fish sold in the U.S., comes from outside of the U.S. When at the counter, we try to buy U.S. fresh-caught and if not, make sure it comes from the U.S. for control purposes. Also, many times when buying fillets of high-priced fish, you may be getting a lower-priced species, as the fillet may be switched from a lower-priced species. Might I add, our all time favorite is halibut.

I will end this section with my synopsis of the book, *French Women Don't Get Fat*, by Mireille Guiliano. It was a wonderful short read and I not only enjoyed it but lost twenty pounds after reading it and have kept it off. I was so enthused about it that I would give talks on it at Rotary.

&. FRENCH WOMEN DON'T GET FAT

Synopsis of the book, *French Women Don't Get Fat* by Mireille Guiliano, by Jim Eiting, March 16, 2008.

The book has little to do with being a woman or being French. Any nationality or sex will get a lot out of it.

As a prelude to the book, I would like to state that my doctor thought it would be a good idea to lose ten pounds. I thought he was kidding as I could still see the tips of my shoes. Well, I ended up losing fifteen pounds because of the book.

In losing weight, you really have to want to or you will not lose any. It starts with mind control that drifts into portion control and that is dictated by discipline and that discipline has to stay with you forever if you want to be and stay slim.

It is not the fat that you see that is dangerous, it is the fat around your internal organs. That fat will also stress your feet and joints and they will begin showing up in your late 50s.

As you age it is easier to gain weight and twice as hard to take it off. Too, being thin makes you look much younger.

From her previous book, *Americans on Average Eat 10% to 30% More Than They Need To Daily*, this connects to the stat of them being 30% above their ideal weight on average.

It is entirely a mental game. French women eat with their heads. You must learn to fool yourself as bodies are machines that can "reset" themselves. Little things do add up.

They always eat with plates that are never covered with food and they never eat standing up. Also, never in front of the television. They chew slowly and well, eating only one thing at a time, but always three meals a day.

Food is a pleasure they really enjoy and realize that the taste actually comes from the first two bites. The same as wine. After the first two swallows, you really never savor the flavor again. They never ever take second helpings. Always small portions. They eat with their five senses.

One half pound of anything is too much! Meat on rare occasions and never more than the size of a deck of cards. They never leave the table feeling stuffed as they feel "The journey is the destination!" If an occasion comes about where they feel that they have eaten too much, they compensate for it the next meal or day.

The essence of French gastronomy is "Have a little of several things vs. a lot of one or two." They eat little bread and never before a meal. Never prepared foods or pastries, bagels, potato chips, pizza, ice cream, candy (dark chocolate only), soda, fruit juices, anything fried. Never beer or hard liquor. They are big on fruits and vegetables. Also, the French are number one in the world on soup consumption. Soups are so good for you in many, many ways. If a snack is in order, a few unsalted nuts (very nutritional).

They drink lots of water all day long and start with a tall glass in the early morning. It keeps you from being hungry and flushes toxins.

They know loss of sleep causes overeating and realize that overeating can be a cause of a deeper problem. They do not lean on their heritage (i.e. heavy parent).

They watch little television and walk a lot. They take the stairs and may take a walk while having to wait on something. They enjoy the environment. They walk and use it as Decompress Time, for a minimum of 20 minutes per day. When walking they imagine a wire attached to the top of their head always pulling it upward so it is always erect and their eyes peer into the distance. Their chin is out and their chest also. Back is straight.

They feel dining in is as great as dining out and enjoy entertaining. If eating out, they feel it is intelligent to split a meal with their partner.

They understand that one does not laugh because one is happy but they are happy because they laugh.

In conclusion, I would like to share some of my personal *tricks*:

- If at Wendy's, I order a small chili and no cheese or for a cheeseburger, get their junior.
- If at Skyline, I order the small portion with light cheese.
- Liking candy, I found that Reese's peanut butter cups to be half peanut butter and that is good for you. I eat half of one where I used to eat a full one.
- I chew lots of sugar-free gum and only one-third of a stick at a time.
- Un-buttered popcorn is very filling and full of fiber.
- Ice cream? Soft serve only and the baby cone size.
- Never sugar, use substitutes.

Finally, I feel good about myself as a result of what I have learned, and that is the name of the game in life.

ON EATING OUT

Having traveled all of our lives, the thrill of eating out is gone. We love cooking in our own home which is fun and very comfortable. At home, you do not have to be concerned about service, noise, temperature, etc. Also, there are no interruptions from people talking about nothing. We also control the calories and amount of spices.

Take-aways have also gained with us. We even get our pizza half-baked and finish them at home, thus the temperature and crispness is certain.

In terms of what time to go to dinner, in addition to the early bird specials, eating early finds the restaurant is quieter, the service is better, and the staff and food are also fresher. Might I add that the specials are many times the uncooked food left over from yesterday.

Finally, this comment made by a family member who worked as a waitress. "To the diner, the tip means very little, but to the server it means everything."

GOURMET CLUBS / DINNER GROUPS

Over the years, we have belonged to quite a few and always enjoyed them, as they are a great way to cement relationships (and drink good wine). A few simple notes:

- A.B.S.—Always Bring Something. Wine is the easy one. Pies, cobblers, etc. get more attention. Hosts love the line, "What can I bring?"
- We have found that the most successful and long-lasting relationships are the ones where the husband likes to cook.
- Very important is using your favorite recipes but choosing one that is cooking while you spend time with your guests over appetizers. (Preparing in the afternoon, like chowders.) Grilling helps in that regard. But, you still have that panic before serving.
- We have always found that a good Port with blue cheese is a nice way to finish off the night.
- And finally this from our son-in-law, Dr. Rob Klamar, "Make sure you wash your wine glasses in the morning... They will last much longer!"

CHEESE

WINE PAIRING: Riesling (for soft cheese), Chardonnay (for hard cheese).

When beginning to write this book, the last thing on my mind was the above. But in the many contacts that I made putting the book together, one of the deepest in the wine trade was Antonio Gardella. One day, he made the comment "cheese amplifies the flavor of wine." Notable too, are combining the two, to create a new taste altogether.

Thus began the pursuit of this chapter. I was very fortunate to know of a specialty cheese store in Santa Barbara by the name of C'est Cheese. The owner of the store, Kathryn Graham, was very helpful to me and suggested the books that I read to flesh it out.

So we must begin with some cheese history which is buried in the monastery history of Europe, as is wine. The monks in the various monasteries, not only had the ambition and patience to make wine but since the climates for both are the same, they went hand in hand with dairy foods. Notable too, are how the terrior of both are compatible and, with milk being eighty percent water, the flavors meld in with the cheese. The same goes with the water and the nutrients in that area. Might I add that the wines of different regions were crafted to compliment the food produced there.

So what about pairing the two? Well the easiest marriage is the dessert wines. This is followed by sparkling, then white and finally reds, which are the most difficult. Important too, is that the cheese flavor should never overpower the wine. Since seventy percent of a wine's taste comes from aroma, with cheese, that aroma figure jumps to ninety percent. That puts a lot of importance of selection and pairing! Along with that, one must balance the salt in the cheese with the sugar in the wine. Noteworthy here is that both contain acid. A few trailing comments on cheese:

- Artisanal (Mom and Pop) cheeses are generally consumed in the general area where they are produced.
- Your harder cheeses (with less water) are aged in caves similar to wine. And again similar, as it ages, the flavors become more concentrated. Some cheeses are aged three to four years.

- Never pre-cut cheeses. To retain flavor, cut as you go, always leaving a portion of the rind.
- And finally, never serve cheese too cold or it loses flavor and aroma. Always allow them to get to room temperature for one hour before serving.

❧ STEAK...THE ALL-AMERICAN CHOICE

WINE PAIRING: Any heavy red wine.

Steak is the traditional all-American choice and probably always will be. We figure one-half pound per couple. A lightly marbleized cut makes for a juicy, tender steak. We like Prime rather than Choice, depending on your budget.

To prepare it, get it to room temperature. Then rub it with sliced fresh garlic, pepper it, and coat it fairly heavily with heavy salt crystals. This will draw protein and create a nice crust as you grill it. Then spray it with olive oil.

Grill it at the hottest temperature possible, turning it only once. You want to sear in the moisture. Once anything gets dry, it also gets tough! Figure five minutes per side as you cannot un-cook anything.

Then place it on a warm (not hot) metal platter for five minutes as you want the juices to flow back through the cut. A nice touch at this point is a small slice of butter.

As an option in inclement weather, lightly coat a cast iron skillet with olive oil and get it as hot as possible adding heavy salt crystals to the bottom of it. Place the steak in the skillet for two minutes per side. Then set the steak aside and get the skillet back to low setting and cook it another two minutes per side. It always works well for us.

In terms of economy, your better cuts such as Porterhouse, fillets, etc. are priced at $12.00–$13.00 per pound. The prices then go down to $7.00 per pound for skirt steak which can be very good or very tough. Skirt steak is commonly used for things such as fajitas.

An inexpensive option that we like is Hangar steak. It is priced around $8.75 per pound. Sometimes called butcher steak, as many times, the butchers kept it for themselves. We cannot find it in supermarkets and call a butcher shop and order two or three one-half pound packages.

The cut is very lean, dark in color, tender and has an intense beef flavor much like fillet. The thickness will vary and it does have a muscle down the center of it and we cook it with the muscle in for flavor. Then we cut around the muscle when we serve it and cut it very thin and against the grain. Depending on the thickness, we grill it about six minutes per side, turning only once.

On a personal note, probably the best piece of beef we have ever had was in Argentina which is known for its good beef. It was in Buenos Aires (good winds), down on the river and the name was Cabaña Las Lilas. To bring the necessity of high heat importance, as you walk into the dining area, you pass the cooking area which I think must have had enough charcoal and heat to melt iron. We actually held out our hands aside of our face to shield the heat. That convinced us of the importance of high heat.

Recipes

🍽 DRY PARMESAN CHEESE CRISPINS

These are for appetizers or garnish for a Caesar Salad. The following is from the chef at the Santa Barbara Yacht Club.
WINE PAIRING: All wines.

INGREDIENTS
1 small package hard Parmesan cheese
Olive oil

METHOD
Shave the Parmesan on parchment paper. Very lightly, spray olive oil on a 15" square cookie sheet. Place shaved cheese in small thin bird's nests on the sheet. Place on top shelf of your oven at 375° for 15 minutes. Remove the lacy cheese nests with spatula. Place in a plastic bag for future use; no need to refrigerate. One cheese package should make approximately 18 cheese nests.

SIMPLE CAESAR SALAD

WINE PAIRING: Sauvignon Blanc

INGREDIENTS

Washed Romaine lettuce (stalky ends)
Garlic cloves
Canned Parmesan
Garlic croûtons
Anchovies
Buttermilk dressing

METHOD

Rub a wooden bowl with garlic cloves liberally. Add the Romaine lettuce. Sprinkle in the Parmesan and add the croûtons. Add cut-up anchovies liberally. Sprinkle with buttermilk dressing. Put in the freezer for ten minutes and then serve. This is a quick and easy recipe for two people.

REDSKIN POTATO CASSEROLE

This recipe is from my older sister, Jan Brinkman.
The dish serves four people.
WINE PAIRING: All wines

INGREDIENTS

8 medium size red potatoes
1 stick butter or margarine, melted

4 green onions, chopped

Fresh parsley

Salt

Pepper

Parmesan cheese

METHOD

Cook the potatoes with skins on in boiling, salted water. Cook until just done, but still firm (do not overcook). Cool and dice potatoes into good-size pieces. Mix with melted butter. Add the green onions, parsley, salt and pepper, and a generous amount of Parmesan cheese. Put in a flat casserole dish and bake for 30–35 minutes. I usually add more Parmesan cheese on top.

EGGPLANT PARMIGIANA

This is from the Inn at Versailles. The dish serves four people.
WINE PAIRING: Chianti Classico

INGREDIENTS

1 medium eggplant

3 garlic cloves

1 medium white onion

¼ bunch fresh parsley

1 small can Contadina tomato paste

½ tsp. basil

1 tsp. oregano

½ cup sun-dried tomatoes

1 tbsp. Brandy

12 oz. mozzarella cheese

2 oz. hard Parmesan cheese

METHOD

Cut the eggplant into ¼ slices. Mince the garlic cloves and the onion. Cut up the fresh parsley. Take the can of Contadina tomato paste and mix with a can of hot water. Add to it the basil and oregano. Dice ½ cup of sun-dried tomatoes.

Over medium heat, sauté the eggplant in olive oil for 5 minutes on each side. Set aside. Sauté the onion, garlic, sun-dried tomatoes, and spices with the Brandy for 10 minutes. Use a fair amount of heat. Add pepper. Add tomato paste mixture and stir in.

In a baking dish with a cover, layer it starting with the tomato mixture, then eggplant slices, parsley, and then add the mozzarella cheese and hard Parmesan. Repeat for 3 layers. Bake at 350° with the lid on for 20 min-

utes. Take the lid off and bake for another 10 minutes, then broil it for 5 minutes.

‑‑

ஃ CABBAGE SOUP WITH SAUSAGE-CHEESE TOASTS

This dish makes six servings.
WINE PAIRING: Riesling

INGREDIENTS

½ cup unsalted butter, softened
2 medium-sized onions, finely chopped
1 small head Savoy cabbage, cored and finely chopped
1 tsp. salt
2 quarts water
12 slices French bread, toasted
12 slices garlic sausage such as Kielbasa
2 cups grated Gruyere cheese
Freshly ground black pepper

METHOD

Melt ¼ cup of the butter in a heavy 4-quart soup pot over very low heat. Add the onions and cabbage, and cook, stirring often, until they begin to take on a golden color, 10 to 12 minutes. Add the salt and water and bring to a boil over high heat. Reduce the heat to low, cover, and simmer for 30 minutes.

Meanwhile, preheat the oven to 450°. Place an ovenproof tureen or deep casserole in the oven to preheat. Spread the slices of French bread with remaining ¼ cup butter and place a round of sausage on each. Sprinkle evenly with the cheese, completely covering the sausage and bread. Press down lightly on the sausage pieces. Put the cheese-sausage croûtes on a baking sheet and bake in the oven until cheese is melted and golden, 4 to 5 minutes. Taste the soup and add more salt if needed and black pepper to taste. Put the hot croûtes in the bottom of the hot tureen or casserole and pour the cabbage-onion soup over them. Cover and serve.

There is a surprise when you ladle this soup into a heated soup tureen lined with the sausage toasts hot from the oven. When the broth contacts the blistering sausages, it sputters and sizzles. This is unexpected and entertaining, but the aroma of the garlic sausage is breathtaking, exactly as French food writer Roger Lallemand describes, "When the maîtresse de maison serves this redolent soup, she removes the cover of the tureen at table and exclaims: 'Vous parlez d'un fumet morvandiau!'"

(Roughly translated: "Talk about garlic sausage!")

❧ REUBEN (SOUP) STEW

This dish serves four people.
WINE PAIRING: Sangiovese

INGREDIENTS
2 cups chicken stock
1½ cups hot, regular milk
⅓ lb. cooked corn beef, cut into ribbons
8 oz. Sauerkraut
3 tbsp. real butter
¼ cup onions
¼ cup celery
3 oz. flour
3 garlic cloves, crushed
¼ tablespoon Worcestershire sauce
Pepper as needed (no salt)

METHOD
Sauté the onions and celery in butter for 10 minutes. Add the flour and make a roux for 10 minutes. Stir with a wire whip. Add the remaining ingredients and cook for 40 minutes with a vented lid. Serve into warm bowls. Per-

haps add a few strips of room temperature Swiss cheese. Croûton may be added if desired.

🐢 MARSHA'S MOCK TURTLE SOUP

This dish serves six people.
WINE PAIRING: Merlot

INGREDIENTS
3 lbs. ground chuck, browned and drained
6 beef bouillon cubes
2 tsp. minced onion
3 (14½ oz.) cans diced tomatoes
1 (12½ oz.) can diced tomatoes with green chilies
¾ cup ketchup
¼ cup brown sugar
¼ cup vinegar, cider or white
1 tsp. black pepper
½ tsp. allspice
½ tsp. ground cloves
¾ stacked crushed crackers
6 hard-cooked eggs, diced fine

METHOD
Simmer the ground chuck and bouillon cubes in 2 quarts of water for one hour. Then add the onion, diced tomatoes, tomatoes with green chilies, ketchup, brown sugar,

vinegar, pepper, allspice, and ground cloves and simmer for one hour. Add the crushed crackers and simmer for another hour. Last, add the diced, hard-cooked eggs.

✿ BOUILLABAISSE

This dish serves eight to ten people.
WINE PAIRING: Chablis

INGREDIENTS

2 cups dry white wine

1 (6 oz.) can minced clams with juice

1 lb. Haddock (or substitute fillets)

1 lb. Cod (or substitute fillets)

6 oz. cooked shrimp (or more), cut up

8 oz. lump crab meat

¼ cup olive oil

1 large onion, coarsely chopped to equal 1 cup

½ cup green onions, chopped

3 garlic cloves, chopped

3 peeled tomatoes, chopped (or 1 lb can without juice)

½ tsp. grated orange rind

2 bay leaves

Saffron, very small amount (⅟₃₂ tsp.)

Pepper, coarse

⅛ lb. butter

1 tsp. bouillon crystals

1 tsp. parsley flakes

1 slice of toast per bowl

Croûtons

METHOD

Pour wine into a heavy kettle. Add all seafood. Add just enough water to cover. Bring to a low boil, covered. Continue boiling on medium, low heat for 10 minutes. Wipe out crud.

In a heavy skillet, add olive oil, onion, green onions, and garlic. Sauté for 10 minutes. Combine kettle contents and skillet contents. Add remaining ingredients except for the toast and croutons. Simmer for 20 minutes, covered. Let stand covered for 10 minutes.

Put toast into preheated bowls and ladle in the soup. Cover with croutons. Serve, smile, mmm!

🍷 CLOIS' FISH CHOWDER

This recipe is from a good Canadian fishing
trip friend. This dish serves six people.

WINE PAIRING: Pinot Noir

INGREDIENTS

1½ lbs. strong fish, such as Northern or Grouper
¼ lb. butter
2 quarts half and half milk
Salt
Pepper
White Pepper
3 red potatoes, diced
1 stalk celery, diced
1 carrot, diced
2 slices raw onion, diced
Milk (optional)

METHOD

Fry fish in butter for 10 minutes on low heat. Cool and debone. Pour butter and drippings into half and half. Add salt, pepper, and white pepper. Add potatoes, celery, carrot, onion, and milk (if desired). Begin cooking uncovered on low-medium heat, and then turn gradually down to warm. Cook for 2 hours. Cooking out the water makes it rich. Too rich? Just add some milk. Serve with oyster crackers.

FELIX'S OYSTER CHOWDER

This recipe was discovered by us in 1970. It was actually gleaned from James Michener's book, Chesapeake, a great book. We named it in honor of a friend from Louisiana who had a father named Felix. This dish serves eight people.

WINE PAIRING: Pinot Noir

INGREDIENTS

48 regular fresh oysters if available (2 pounds); set aside the oyster "liquor" until later

¾ lb. bacon, cut up, 4 pieces per slice

2 quarts half and half milk

1 large white onion, chopped

3 stalks celery, chopped

¼ lb. butter, cut into squares

1 tbsp. minute tapioca

Dash of white pepper

Dash of salt

Dash of Worcestershire sauce

Dash of Old Bay seafood seasoning

Few sprigs of fresh or dried parsley

METHOD

Fry the bacon but do not crisp and set aside. Drain off and discard half the grease. In a pot, begin heating the half and half. In the remaining bacon grease, sauté the onions and celery. Remove them to the half and half. Keep the grease in the skillet. In the remaining bacon grease, gently fry the oysters until the gills wrinkle. Place the oysters and remaining liquid left in the skillet into the half and half cooking pot. Add tapioca and butter and oyster liquor to the cooking pot. Simmer the pot for 1 hour with lid partially on. Reduce heat. Oyster crackers are optional. This chowder is very rich. It actually does get better on the second day.

✎ ESCARGOT CHOWDER WITH GARLIC

This dish serves four people.
WINE PAIRING: Prosecco

INGREDIENTS

3 dozen escargots, cut in half
¼ cup butter
1 medium-sized onion, finely chopped
2 young carrots, finely chopped
1 leek, white and pale white only, halve it then thinly slice
¾ quart chicken broth, not low fat
7 garlic cloves, minced
Salt
Pepper
¾ quart half and half milk
1 cup fresh parsley
Tiny herbal croûtons

METHOD

Rinse and trim snails. Melt butter in a heavy 4-quart sauce pan over medium heat. Add the onions, carrots, leek, and snails. Cook covered for 10 minutes.

Add garlic, broth, salt, and pepper. Bring to a low boil over high heat. Reduce to very low heat. Cover partially for 30 minutes. Add the half and half milk and return to a brief boil. Turn back to low heat with no lid for 30 minutes.

Heat the bowls in the oven. Upon serving, ladle into heated bowls and sprinkle with fresh parsley. Use croûtons if desired. Reheated the next night it tastes even better.

🐌 POACHING

For halibut, sea bass, escolar, etc. This recipe is for two people. Figure ¼ pound or less per person.

WINE PAIRING: Pinot Grigio

INGREDIENTS

1 carrot

1 stalk celery

½ sweet white onion

1 garlic clove, diced

1 bouillon cube

Thyme

Parsley

1 bay leaf

METHOD

In a covered cooking pan, combine half white wine and half water about 1½" deep, so it will cover ¾ of the fillet. The fillet should be skin-on, room temperature, and with salt and pepper.

Cut thin and lengthwise the carrot, celery, and onion and mix with the garlic. Place these, without the fillet, in the pot and lightly boil for 30 minutes with the lid half on. Add salt and pepper and drop in the bouillon cube, thyme, parsley, and bay leaf. Then cook with the fillet for 12–15 minutes on low heat with the lid on. Cook everything together with the lid on and low heat for 20–30 minutes. The fish will begin to separate. Lift out the veggies with a slotted spoon, remove the skin from the fillet, and serve together. It is nice to have the bowls heated if possible. You may want to freeze the roux for next time.

&. BAKED COD OR GROUPER WITH GRAND MARNIER AND ORANGE SLICES

This dish serves two people.
WINE PAIRING: Viognier

INGREDIENTS

½ lb. fish
Grand Marnier sauce
Orange slices

METHOD

Salt and pepper the fish and place in a baking dish sprayed with olive oil. Spread the fish generously with butter and drip with Grand Marnier. Place orange slices on top of the fish. Place in the oven uncovered at 350° for 35 minutes total. At 20 minutes, drip more Grand Marnier over the fish. Return to oven for the last 15 minutes.

🐟 HALIBUT, SNAPPER, OR GROUPER WITH GRAPES AND WALNUTS

This dish serves two people.

WINE PAIRING: Chardonnay

INGREDIENTS

½ lb. of fillet

½ cup of white and red grapes, halved

¼ cup of walnuts, halved

3 cloves of garlic, peeled and sliced lengthwise

2 tablespoons butter

Sea salt

Ground pepper

Thyme

METHOD

Preheat oven to 400°. Place fillets in a small baking dish over a light coating of olive oil. Mix grapes, walnuts, garlic, and butter with salt, pepper, and thyme into a small skillet and melt/mix over low heat.

Pour ¾ contents of skillet over fish and place in the oven covered for 20 minutes. Then baste with the skillet contents and bake for 10 minutes more. Put leftovers in a container and move it to the table.

PARMESAN ENCRUSTED SOLE WITH SAUTÉED FRESH SPINACH

This recipe comes from the restaurant McCormick & Schmick's. This dish serves two people.

WINE PAIRING: White blend

INGREDIENTS
1 bag fresh spinach
¼ lb. Sole per person
Flour
Parmesan cheese
Pine nuts

METHOD
Sautée the spinach at medium heat in butter and olive oil for 2–3 minutes. Set aside in warm oven with serving plates. Dust the sole in flour and fry them at me-

dium/high heat for 4 minutes per side in the same skillet with butter and olive oil. Use pepper but no salt. The cheese is high in salt.

Place the sole on top of spinach in skillet and dust the sole with fresh grated Parmesan cheese. Top with a few pine nuts. Place under broiler for 4 minutes until cheese is browned a bit. Keep in mind that the sole is a most delicate fish, so watch the heat.

SALMON WITH LEEK FOR TWO
WINE PAIRING: Pinot Noir

INGREDIENTS
½ lb. salmon
1 full stem of leek
3 medium red potatoes

METHOD
Cut salmon into two pieces. Salt and pepper it. Cut the leek into medium slices, white portion only. Dice the red potatoes. Melt ¼ stick of butter and add olive oil to a cast iron skillet. Set on medium heat or less. Cook your red potatoes for 10 minutes. Then add the salmon and cook for 5 minutes. Turn over after 2½ minutes. Finally, add the leek and cook for 10 more minutes covered and vented. Place the skillet on the table and serve.

🐚 OYSTERS ROCKEFELLER

This dish serves four people.
WINE PAIRING: Chardonnay

INGREDIENTS

8 medium-sized oysters per person, on the
    ½ shell or equivalent
2 boxes of chopped frozen spinach, squeeze out moisture
³/₈ lb. butter
4 green onion tops
Small amount of fresh parsley
Small amount of fresh celery leaves
2 crushed garlic cloves
1 tbsp. real mustard
1 tbsp. Pernod
1 tbsp. Bac-Os
1 tbsp. Worcestershire sauce
Pepper

METHOD

Bring all ingredients to a boil except for the oysters. Cover. Stir often and bring to almost a (rough) purée. Turn down to medium/low heat for 30 minutes. Place oysters in shells and cover with purée in a huge oven-proof pan. Heavily dust with Parmesan. Cook for 15 minutes at 450°.

🐚 BOURBON-BRAISED TURKEY LEGS AND THIGHS

This dish serves two people.
WINE PAIRING: All wines

INGREDIENTS
¼ cup Canola or vegetable oil
Unsmoked turkey leg and thigh, remove skin and fat
1 carrot cut into 1" pieces
1 small onion diced into big pieces
1 celery stalk cut into 1" pieces
4 small red potatoes diced into big pieces
1½ garlic cloves
Salt and pepper to taste
¼ cup Bourbon
4 cups chicken stock
2 sprigs fresh thyme

METHOD
In a Dutch oven, place turkey in oil, dusted with flour and salt and pepper. Brown on all sides for 5 minutes at medium heat, set aside. At medium heat, add carrots,

onion, celery, garlic, and thyme. Cook for 5 minutes. Add Bourbon and cook for 2 minutes. Add chicken stock and bring to a simmer for 5 minutes.

Add turkey and cover, place in oven, covered, at 300° for 2 hours. Add potatoes 45 minutes before dish is finished. Dish from Dutch oven at the table. Remove the veggies with a slotted spoon. Eat with sopping bread.

🕊 DUCK A L'ORANGE

This dish serves four people.
WINE PAIRING: Côtes du Rhône

INGREDIENTS
4 duck legs, trim all fat
Salt
Pepper
2 oranges, cut into slices
Grand Mariner sauce
Butter

METHOD
Preheat oven to 400°. Spray baking dish with olive oil. Rub duck all over with butter. Place half of the orange slices in bottom of the dish. Place duck over slices. Bake for ½ hour in oven center,

covered. Remove and drizzle duck with Grand Mariner and add last ½ of orange slices on top. Place back in the oven for 15 minutes. Remove and drizzle duck again with Grand Mariner. Place back in the over for the final 15 minutes. Serve with the orange slices. Total time: 1 hour.

COQ AUBERGE FOR TWO

This dish serves two people.
WINE PAIRING: Red blend

INGREDIENTS
½ lean, 3 lb. broiler chicken, cut the long way through
    (by the butcher's saw)
3 small red potatoes
½ sweet onion in pieces
2 apples, split
1 garlic toe, halved, long way
Few small carrots, sliced long way
Few seedless white grapes
Few green olives

METHOD
Spray a baking dish with olive oil and cover later. Put the chicken in the baking dish along with all other ingredients. Cover and bake at 375° for one hour. This is a very simple, fast, and delicious dinner!

ROSEMARY CHICKEN WITH BALSAMIC TOMATOES

This is from Paula Deen's "The Lighter Side."
This dish serves four people.
WINE PAIRING: Sauvignon Blanc

INGREDIENTS

2 tsp. olive oil

4 chicken cutlets, sliced thin

2 tsp. fresh rosemary, chopped

½ tsp. coarsely ground black pepper

1 small red onion, thinly sliced

2 garlic cloves, minced

2 tsp. balsamic vinegar

2 cups grape tomatoes, halved

¼ cup reduced sodium chicken broth

Pinch of salt

¼ cup fresh basil, chopped

2 tsp. grated orange zest

METHOD

Heat oil in a large non-stick skillet over medium/high heat. Sprinkle the chicken with the rosemary and pepper. Add the cutlets and cook 2–3 minutes on each side. Transfer the chicken to a plate.

Add onion and garlic to the skillet and cook, stirring occasionally, over medium heat until onion is tender. Add the vinegar and cook, stirring occasionally, until vinegar is almost evaporated. Stir in the tomatoes, broth, and salt. Cook, stirring often, until the tomatoes begin to soften and the sauce begins to thicken slightly, about 5 minutes. Stir in basil and orange zest.

Return the chicken and any juices to the skillet and heat through. Place one cutlet on each of 4 plates. Top with ⅓ cup tomato mixture. This is a very easy and fast recipe. Also, if cooking for only 2, refrigerate leftovers overnight and add angel hair pasta when reheating. It makes a great leftover meal reinvigorated.

BEEF WELLINGTON

This is a special family recipe used for Esther's birthday which is Christmas Eve. This dish serves eight people.
WINE PAIRING: Cabernet Sauvignon

INGREDIENTS
5 lb. tenderloin of beef
3 oz. mushrooms, diced fine
3 tbsp. Brandy
Pâté foie gras
Puff pastry
1 egg, beaten

METHOD

Bake beef for 25 minutes at 425°. Remove from oven and take off all the fat and casing. It should have an internal temperature of 120°.

Place in a skillet with 3 tablespoons of butter, mushrooms, and Brandy. Cook until liquid is almost gone. Mix with pâté foie gras.

Roll out puff pastry and put contents of skillet into it so you can wrap it evenly around the tenderloin. Brush with beaten egg. Return to oven and bake for 20 minutes at 425° on a middle shelf. Lower to 375° and bake for another 20 minutes. Internal temperature should be 120°. Remove and allow it to stand for 15 minutes. Cut into ¾ inch slices. Serve with au jus.

ESTHER'S YANKEE POT ROAST

This dish serves six people, but it is also wonderful warmed up the following day.

WINE PAIRING: Merlot

INGREDIENTS

1 (2½ lb.) boneless beef chuck shoulder pot roast

⅓ cup all-purpose flour

¾ tsp. salt

¾ tsp. black ground pepper

1 tbsp. vegetable oil

1 (14 oz.) can beef broth

½ cup dry red wine

1½ tsp dried thyme leaves

1 tsp. tarragon

2 packs (16 oz.) frozen vegetable stew mixture
    (potatoes, carrots, celery, and onions)

METHOD

Combine flour, salt, and pepper. Lightly coat beef in 2 tablespoons of flour mixture. Heat oil in large stockpot and brown evenly. Pour off drippings. Combine beef broth, red wine, thyme, tarragon, and remaining flour to stockpot. Bring to a boil. Reduce heat to simmer and cover for 2 hours. Add the vegetables and continue simmering for 45 minutes until tender. Remove stockpot and skim fat. Keep warm. Carve pot roast into thin slices and serve with vegetables and gravy. On the lighter side, we had a dear friend by the name of Corrinne Francis who had a small dog by the name of "Pot Roast!"

🐌 LONDON BROIL FOR FOUR

WINE PAIRING: Bordeaux Reserve

INGREDIENTS

Large flank steak

1½ garlic cloves, crushed

Salt

Pepper

¼ stick butter

1 lb. fresh mushrooms, sliced

2 tbsp. flour

1 can beef consommé

½ cup dry white wine

2 green onions, chopped (including tops)

Pinch of thyme

Pinch of Parsley

Bay leaf

METHOD

Let steak warm to room temperature. Crisscross the steak with shallow slashes. Rub with 1 crushed garlic clove. Season with salt and pepper and let it sit for 30 minutes.

Sauté mushrooms in butter. Pour some of the liquid off. Add to liquid the flour, beef consommé, wine, ½ crushed garlic clove, green onions, thyme, parsley, and bay leaf. Salt and pepper as desired and simmer over low heat for ½ hour. Stir as needed, cover if desired.

Broil or grill the steak as you like it. When finished, place on hot platter and slice diagonally against the grain in thin strips. Pour sauce over steaks and serve.

🐌 EPILOGUE

The good fortune and serendipity related to my wine and food experiences mimic those of my life, in general. I feel like I am one lucky fellow. Reaching out to friends, sharing a myriad of experiences in this country and around the world, finding myself in a variety of unusual situations—they have all added to my passion for sharing my thoughts for this book.

I learned early in my international travels that port cities were most interesting as they were filled with people from many nations and thus places where knowledge intersected. Similar to computers and databases today, they are where knowledge collects and multiplies.

Each year, I share six bullet points with our six wonderful grandchildren, to help them with their education.

Esther and I with our family celebrating the 100th anniversary of Midmark Corporation at the Grand Hotel on Mackinac Island.

Last year, one was: "When invited to an event, say hi to all of your friends, but sit with the people you don't know, as their knowledge of other things will help you build your personal database of knowledge."

The same might be said for discovering the world of wine: "Don't get stuck on one varietal. Reach out and try others and build your base of knowledge. In time, you will find your personal *sweet spot*."

I had a great deal of fun writing this book. I hope you will have the same reading it.

Finally, this gem: most people are remembered until the death of their youngest grandchild; authors are remembered forever.

🍇 GLOSSARY

Acidity: Vitally needed to give wines freshness, zest, snap, and longevity.

Aperitif: Any drink drunk before eating, ostensibly to induce appetite.

Astringent: A dry quality causing the mouth to pucker. Usually from high tannin or acid.

Buttery: A flavor associated with white wines only; usually California Chardonnays. This phenomenon comes from malolactic fermentation.

Chaptalization: The addition of sugar during fermentation to boost the alcohol percentage.

Cuvée: Contents of a vat or quantity of blended wine.

Dry: The opposite of sweet wines.

Fermentation: Conversion of grape juice into wine through the action of certain yeasts present in the juice, which turns sugar into alcohol.

Fining: A method of clarifying wine by adding a coagulant such as egg whites.

Flute: A tall, narrow cone-shaped glass for sparkling wines.

Fortified: A wine strengthened by adding additional alcohol during production.

Grand Cru: The best category of wine.

Hydrometer: An instrument that determines the brix of sugar during fermentation.

In vino veritas: In wine, truth.

Late harvest: Wines made from grapes with extensive "hang time," thus increased sweetness.

Jug wine: Table wine or wine by the growler. Cheap work day wine.

Legs: Rivulets or church windows created by the alcohol running down the side of the glass.

Magnum: Large wine bottle holding 1½ liters, equivalent of two normal bottles.

Maceration: Fermentation process where the phenolic materials of the grape—tannins, coloring agents, and flavor compounds—are leached from the grape skins, seeds, and stems into the must.

Malolactic fermentation: A secondary fermentation process to mellow the wine flavor.

Oxidized: Excessive exposure to air; causes a stale, flat taste to the wine.

Pasteurization: Heat introduction for sterilization; used for some common wines.

Phylloxera: A pest causing the vines to die. It almost wiped out vines worldwide in the 19th century. Now vines are grafted to prevent it.

Plonk: Slang for everyday wine.

Punt: The hollow in the bottom of a wine bottle. Used less frequently today.

Resveratrol: A natural fungicide found on the skin of red grapes, blueberries, etc. Reputed to be healthgiving.

Rouge: French for red.

Ruby: Young port wine aged very little.

Sommelier: (pronounced SOM-EL-YA) The chief wine steward in a fine restaurant.

Spritzer: A mixture of white wine and soda water.

Spumante: Italian for sparkling.

Sulphur: Disinfectant dusted on vines to prevent fungus. Also, added to the must of wine in the form of sulphur dioxide to destroy harmful bacteria.

Tartaric: Acid occurring naturally in grapes. That is where the acid mainly comes from.

Ullage: The air space in the neck of a full wine bottle.

Varietal: Indicates the type of grape used in fermentation. For a label to carry that name, it means that at least 95% of those grapes came from that year.

Yeast: Collection of micro-organisms which causes fermentation. Wild yeasts are naturally present on grape skins but special yeasts are also usually used.

🕭 CONVERSION TABLES

VOLUME

Standard wine bottle = 0.75 liter (l) / 750 milliliters (ml) / 75 centiliters (cl)

1 liquid pint = 0.473 liter

1 quart = 0.946 liter

1 gallon = 3.785 liters

1 hectoliter (hl) = 100 liters = 26.4 gallons

1 barrique = 60 gallons = 225 liters = 300 bottles

1 tonneau = 4 barriques = 900 liters = 1,200 bottles

1 liter = 2.114 liquid pints

1 liter = 1.057 quarts

1 liter = 0.264 gallon

AREA

1 acre = 0.405 hectare

1 hectare = 2.47 acres

10 hectares is nearly 25 acres (1 hectare = 10,000 sq. meters = 2.47 acres)

10 acres is just over 4 hectares (1 acre = 4,840 sq. yards = 0.405 hectare)

5,000 vines per hectare is approximately 2,000 per acre

🐚 INDEX

A

acidity, 5–6, 16, 59, 62–63, 67–68
Ackert, Sid, 43, 46
aging, 8–9, 20–21, 36, 50, 58
Airen, 79
alcohol percentages, 13–14
alkalinity, 5
Alsatian sculptures, 38
Americans on Average Eat 10 to 30% More Than They Need To Daily (Guiliano), 87
American wines, overview of, 71–72
antioxidants, 52
Aperitif, 69–70, 125
Argentina, 63, 75, 94
Armagnac, 58
Ashley's vineyard, 46
Australia, 19, 70, 75
Azerbaijan, 4

B

Baked Cod or Grouper with Grand Marnier and Orange Slices, 109–110
Beef Wellington, 118–119
Bien Nacido vineyard, 46
Black Sea, 4, 47
blending, 24–25, 62, 67
Bordeaux, xi, 9, 26, 41, 56–59, 67–69, 72, 74, 77, 120
Bouillabaisse, 103–104
Bourbon-Braised Turkey Legs and Thighs, 114–115
Boys Club, 46
Braille Institute, 46
brandy, 58
Brinkman, Jan, 96
Brut, 60
Burgundy, 58–59, 62, 64, 74, 77
Buttonwood vineyard, 46

C

Cabaña Las Lilas, 94
Cabbage Soup with Sausage-Cheese Toasts, 99–101
Cabernet Franc, 45, 56, 58, 79
Cabernet Sauvignon, 20, 37, 45, 56, 58–59, 63, 68, 73–76, 79, 118
California State Fair, 46
California wines, overview of, 72–73
California, xi–xiii, 7, 12, 19, 21, 28, 39, 42, 45–46, 57, 59, 64, 69–74, 125
Canada, 38, 62, 76
Cascade Mountains, 73
Caspian Sea, 4
Catawba Peninsula, 12
Caucasus, 4
C'est Cheese, 91
Chablis, 59–60, 103
Champagne, 9, 60–61, 77
chaptalization, 36, 78
Chardonnay, 6, 37, 58–61, 69–70, 73–74, 76, 91, 110, 113
Chateau d'Yquem, 68
cheese, 18, 29, 52, 66, 89–93, 95, 97–100, 102, 111–112
Chenin Blanc, 61, 79
Chesapeake (Michener), 106
Chianti, 68, 78, 97
Chief Executive magazine, free enterprise system in Eastern Europe and Russia, 47
Child, Julia, 38–39
Chile, 19, 76
Christian Brothers winery, 37
Christie's auction, 41
Claret, 56
Clois' Fish Chowder, 105
Cognac, 58
Colheita, 65